W9-DFU-847

SHOW OF HANDS

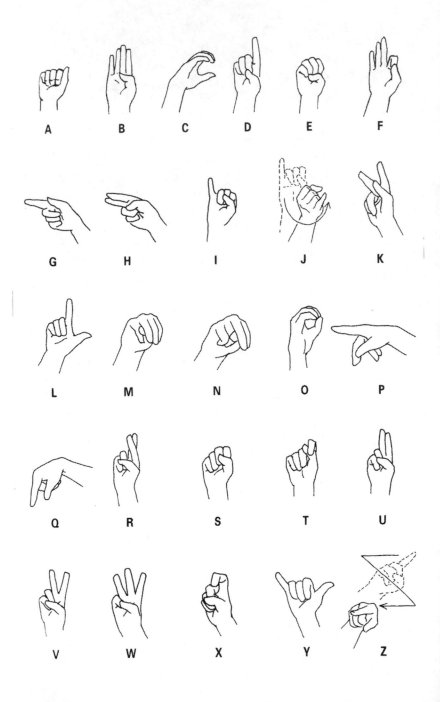

A B C D E F

G H I J K

L M N O P

Q R S T U

V W X Y Z

SHOW
OF
HANDS

A Natural
History of
Sign Language

David F. Armstrong

Gallaudet University Press | *Washington, DC*

Gallaudet University Press
Washington, DC 20002
http://gupress.gallaudet.edu

© 2011 by Gallaudet University
All rights reserved. Published 2011. Second printing 2012.
Printed in the United States of America

Cover art from Jean-Baptiste Carpeaux's sculpture *Ugolino*, photographed
by Vassil Asjac. Courtesy of the photographer.

Frontispiece from Richard A. Tennant and Marianne Gluszak Brown,
The American Sign Language Handshape Starter: A Beginner's Guide, 10.
Washington, D.C.: Gallaudet University Press. Illustration by Valerie
Nelson-Metlay.

Library of Congress Cataloging-in-Publication Data

Armstrong, David F.
    Show of hands : a natural history of sign language / David F. Armstrong.
      p. cm.
    Includes bibliographical references and index.
    ISBN-13: 978-1-56368-488-3 (pbk. : alk. paper)
    ISBN-10: 1-56368-488-8 (pbk. : alk. paper)
    ISBN-13: 978-1-56368-487-6 (electronic book)
    ISBN-10: 1-56368-487-X (electronic book)
      1. Sign language.   2. Sign language—History.   3. Gesture.
    4. Language and languages—Origin.   I. Title.
    HV2474.A76 2011
    419.09—dc22
                                                    2011000862

⊗ The paper used in this publication meets the minimum
requirements of American National Standard for Information
Sciences—Permanence of Paper for Printed Library Materials,
ANSI Z39.48–1984.

Contents

Figures

Acknowledgments

THIS BOOK IS lovingly dedicated to all those friends, deaf and hearing, living and dead, who have made the unique and wonderful world known as Gallaudet and to my family: Vicki, Denise, and Laura. I would especially like to recognize the contributions of my Gallaudet colleagues, co-authors, and co-editors—Vic Van Cleve, and, of course, the late William C. Stokoe. Some of the material in this book is adapted from material I have previously published individually or with my friends and colleagues Sherman Wilcox and Michael Karchmer, and I greatly appreciate their consent to its use here. This book owes much to all of these individuals, and, in particular, it celebrates the fiftieth anniversary of Stokoe's groundbreaking *Sign Language Structure* that launched a revolution in our understanding of human language. Finally, I would like to express my appreciation to the staff of the Gallaudet University Press for all the support I have received from them through the years as author, editor, and director.

1 | Seeing Is Believing

A CONSTELLATION OF anatomical and social peculiarities distinguish human beings from other mammals. These anatomical attributes include upright posture with a striding bipedal gait; relative hairlessness; a brain that is large in comparison to the size of the rest of the body; aspects of the dentition and the anatomy of the jaw and throat; and, most significantly for purposes of this book, an exceptionally dexterous hand with full opposability of the thumb to the other digits. It is particularly instructive to look at these anatomical peculiarities in comparison with similar attributes of our closest living relatives, the higher primates—in particular the great apes of Africa. We will also consider the social arrangements of these primates as they compare to those of humans—in this regard, we will be particularly concerned with the need for complex and often subtle communication systems that support flexible and dynamic small-group interactions.

History of the Human Hand

Why start a book about human sign languages with a discussion of our relationships to our primate relatives? Human beings have long indulged in speculation about the origins of their languages. Visible gesture and the signed languages of the deaf have, as we will see, figured prominently is this speculative literature. Because some scholars have argued that the original human languages were gestural or signed languages, as we

1

attempt to reconstruct their histories it is worth returning to the beginnings of the human lineage. However, this book does not explicitly make the argument for a gestural origin of human language. That has been done elsewhere by a number of authors, including this one. This book illustrates the important ways in which these visible languages have enriched human culture in general and shows how their study has expanded knowledge of the human condition, from the point of view of the Western intellectual tradition in particular.

Human visible gestures can involve virtually all parts of the human body that can be seen by a person's interlocutor, and it is now well known that this is equally true of the sign languages of deaf people—languages that were once referred to as "manual." It is important, therefore, to explain why this book takes the apparently anachronistic approach of concerning itself primarily with the expression of those languages through symbolic activity of the hands. It is argued here that these symbolic activities have a special importance in the expression of signed languages and a significance in human culture that frequently rises to a mystical level. This is simply because of the hand's dexterousness, as mentioned above. The hand is capable of degrees of contrast with respect to symbolic distinctions that gestural behavior involving other parts of the body, for example through changes in facial expression, is not.

Symbolism involving the hands, especially the distinction between the right and the left hand, is ubiquitous in human culture and was a focus of early cross-cultural anthropological research. What this pan-cultural symbolic attribution highlighted, of course, is another uniquely human trait—handedness—and the predominance of the right hand in particular. Although there may be precursors to human handedness among the African apes (see figure 1), nothing exists in the

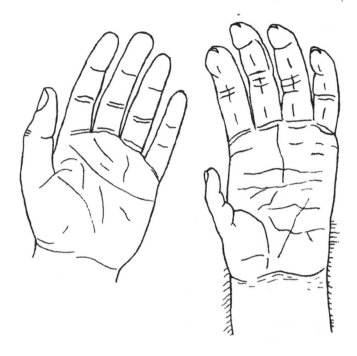

Fig. 1. Hands of human and chimpanzee. Illustration by Robert C. Johnson.

nonhuman primate world that approaches the universal development of skilled behavior by the right hand among modern human populations. It has been known, moreover, since the work of the French anthropologist, Paul Broca, in the nineteenth century, that handedness and aspects of the production of spoken language generally depend upon structures in the left cerebral cortex of the human brain.

As early as 1909, the French sociologist, Robert Hertz, attempted to account for aspects of the cross-cultural right/left dual symbolism by reference to Broca's work on the neurology of handedness and language. What is striking about this cross-cultural literature is the near universal association of the right with positive and the left with negative attributes. In English, the word *dexterous* comes directly from the Latin word for right, while *sinister* is derived from Latin for left. From cross-cultural studies of right/left symbolism compiled by the anthropologist Rodney Needham (1973), we find such widely distributed associations as these:

- Right—strong, social order, senior, esteemed, auspicious, life, eating
- Left—weak, disorder, junior, hated, inauspicious, death, eliminating

Hertz sums up the difference in the following terms:

> What resemblance more perfect than that between our two hands! And yet what a striking inequality there is! To the right hand go honors, flattering designations, prerogatives: it acts, orders, and takes. The left hand, on the contrary, is despised and reduced to the role of humble auxiliary: by itself it can do nothing; it helps, it supports, it holds. (1973, 3)

How, then, did the hand, especially the right hand, come to occupy such a central place in so many aspects of human behavior? In his influential book, *The Hand: How Its Use Shapes the Brain, Language, and Human Culture,* the neurologist Frank Wilson summarizes the essential anatomical adaptations of the primates that made them successful tree dwellers:

1. orbits and eyes moved to a forward position in the head, permitting binocular vision, certainly an advantage for navigating in three-dimensional space and for finding and catching small prey at close distances;
2. forearm and collarbone structure were modified to permit greater flexibility and perhaps greater safety in arboreal travel and dining;

3. paws that retained the archaic but extremely useful five-ray (pentadactyl) pattern, permitting the animal to grasp with individual digits; toes and thumbs acquired the ability to close the gap between the thumb and first digit (i.e., they became convergent, though not yet opposable); nails replaced claws on the dorsal surface of terminal digits, while palmar surfaces acquired sensitive, ridged pulps—all these changes permitted improved climbing and locomotion along trunks and branches, and better grasping and holding of fruits, leaves, and insects;

4. the snout shortened, vision began to supersede smell as the dominant sense, and jaws, skull, and teeth changed, consistent with dietary change;

5. the brain changed in size and configuration, probably to accommodate the geometrically more complex living and hunting environment. (1998, 19–20)

The central thesis of Wilson's book is that the nexus implied here between powerful binocular vision and hands capable of fine manipulation set the stage for the eventual evolution of human beings as makers and users of tools and as successful communicators through visible gesture. Within the primate order, it was human beings who took greatest advantage of this potential for coordinated activity involving hand and eye.

At some point during the evolutionary history of the primates, the hominoids, the superfamily to which humans and apes belong, developed a further specialization related to locomotion. This has been called brachiation or brachiation with "knuckle-walking." This mode of locomotion involves hands with relatively long, hooklike fingers and short thumbs. Apes can thus move through trees by arm-over-arm swinging or by grasping tree limbs from underneath with their hooklike hands and prehensile feet, rather than by running along the upper surfaces of branches like monkeys. On the ground, apes, especially chimps and gorillas that spend much of their time out of the trees, walk on the knuckles of their hands, not the palmar surfaces. However, given their elongated fingers and short thumbs, apes have difficulty bringing their thumbs into full opposition with the palmar surfaces of their fingers—thus, limiting the extent to which they can form precision grips, a hallmark of the human hand.

We should, then, look closely at the anatomy and function of the human hand, within the context of its recent evolutionary history. Very early in the hominid (now often referred to as the hominin) lineage, the lineage leading to modern humans, the evidence concerning the evolution of the hand indicates that the following functional capabilities, characteristic of modern humans, seem to have emerged:

- the thumb, index, and middle fingers can form a "three-jaw chuck," which means the hand can conform to, grasp, and firmly retain irregular solid shapes (such as stones);
- finer control can be exerted over objects held between the thumb and the tips of the index and middle fingers;
- rocks can be held within the hand to pound repeatedly on other objects (nuts, for example), or to dig for roots, because the new wrist structure is able to absorb (dissipate) the shock of repeated hard strikes more effectively than in the ape hand. (Wilson 1998, 26)

As was alluded to above, it is not only the configuration of the hand itself that is significant, but also the neurological specialization of handedness that establishes the unique functional capabilities of human hands. Although some variation in published estimates exists, clearly the vast majority of modern

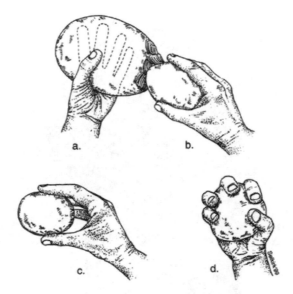

Fig. 2. Human grips. Reproduced with permission from Marzke and Marzke 2000. © John Wiley and Sons.

human beings, up to 90 percent, are right handed—showing a strong preference for using the right hand to perform most skilled activities. Some evidence for handedness in nonhuman primates has been found, not surprisingly among chimpanzees in particular (Hopkins 1999), but most scientists accept that the degree of preference and the prevalence of the right as the preferred hand constitute a uniquely human trait.

This sort of manual dexterity allows humans to use their hands to mimic and thereby represent all sorts of objects and actions. Two downward pointing fingers making a scissoring action can represent a person walking, for example, and five wiggling fingers can represent a spider or other animal. Some of these gestures may be understood almost universally. The 'L' hand held with the finger pointing out and the thumb point-

Fig. 3. Chimpanzee grips. Top photo reproduced with permission from Marzke and Marzke 2000. © John Wiley and Sons. Bottom photo reproduced with permission of the Michale E. Keeling Center for Comparative Medicine and Research, Department of Veterinary Sciences, The University of Texas MD Anderson Cancer Center.

ing up represents a handgun anywhere in the world where such weapons exist. The 'Y' had held with the pinky at the chin and the thumb at the ear represents a telephone everywhere there are telephones. And so on. No other part of the human anatomy is capable of creating signs with this degree of distinctiveness.

Seeing and Hearing

One of the most delightful scenes in all of theater is the play within the play in *A Midsummer Night's Dream* that the Athenian menials present to Duke Theseus and his Amazonian bride, Hippolyta (act V, scene 1). In the middle of this farce, Bottom the weaver, as Pyramus, addresses his beloved Thisbe, who has been speaking on the other side of a Wall: "I see a voice: now will I to the chink, To spy an I can hear my Thisbe's face." Now, as with so much in Shakespeare, this passage has been treated as more than the author intended it to be—a gentle burlesque replete with malapropisms. The first part of Pyramus's line, "I see a voice," has inspired the titles of at least two books about deafness and deaf people: Oliver Sacks's (1989) *Seeing Voices* and a more recent philosophical work by Jonathan Rée (1999) entitled, simply enough, *I See a Voice*. There is some fairly obvious symbolism here that we don't need to dwell on—of course when we see deaf people signing, we are in some way seeing their "voices." Instead, it would be worthwhile to consider the second part of Pyramus's line—"To spy an I can hear my Thisbe's face." Just as we can see the voices of deaf people as they sign, so, equally, can we "hear" faces, assuming of course that we can hear at all. Consider this quotation from another familiar classic of English literature, Dickens's *Christmas Carol:*

> Oh! But he was a tight-fisted hand at the grindstone, Scrooge! A squeezing, wrenching, grasping, scraping, clutching, covetous old sinner! Hard and sharp as flint, from which no steel had ever struck out generous fire; secret, and self-contained, and solitary as an oyster. The cold within him froze his old features, nipped his pointed nose, shriveled his cheek, stiffened his gait; made his eyes red, his thin lips blue; and spoke out shrewdly in his grating voice. A frosty rime was on his head, and on his eyebrows, and his wiry chin. He carried his own

low temperature always about with him; he iced his office in
the dog-days, and he didn't thaw it one degree at Christmas.
(chapter 1)

Only one species of creature alive on Earth is capable of doing what Dickens does here—cause us to construct a visual
image of old Scrooge simply by describing his appearance. In
this case through writing—but the description works equally
well, or perhaps better, when delivered in spoken words.

Psychologists have written much about the importance
of what may be another uniquely human neurological attri-
bute—cross-modal association, the ability to freely combine
sensory input from more than one modality, that is, vision,
hearing, and sense of the body, into higher order concepts and
images. It can be argued that a primary function of metaphor
and other figurative spoken language is to enable the translation of essentially visual information into the abstraction that
sound is to us. Not surprisingly, the only other mammal that
seems to share this ability with us, again if only minimally, may
be the chimpanzee. Cross-modal transfer of sensory information is associated with the cortex of the parietal lobe, one
of the parts of the brain that has grown dramatically during
the course of human evolution. This functional region is also
sometimes referred to as the POT—parietal/occipital/tem-
poral area. But why would this sort of sensory integration be
so important to the appearance of human language?

One of the many curious things about language is that for
most people it is not expressed and perceived in the dominant
human sensory modality, which, unquestionably, is vision. We
are primates, and because we are primates, when we gather
information about the world, we gather it primarily through
our eyes. Primates are so visually oriented presumably because
their ancestors' primary adaptation was arboreal, that is to life

in the trees. Why would vision be so important to animals that live in trees? Armstrong, Stokoe, and Wilcox (1995, 48) have noted a very simple, very draconian Darwinian explanation— a leaping monkey that misses its grip is likely to be a dead monkey. This mode of life, especially when it involves feeding on small food items such as insects and fruits, also requires a great deal of manual dexterity and eye-hand coordination, all of which, as we have seen, are hallmarks of the primate adaptation.

Because we are so visually oriented, it is hard for us to imagine the sensory capabilities of some other animals. When we want to know the truth about a crime, we *look* for an *eyewitness* who *saw* it done. We tend not to accept *hearsay. Seeing,* after all, is believing. But if we were carnivores and not primates, we would probably want to sniff out a nose-witness. Just as we cannot *picture* how a dog constructs its olfactory world, we find it similarly hard to *visualize* the way in which a bat or a dolphin is able to detect the shapes of distant objects using its auditory sense, through a process called *echolocation.* In this case, the sounds perceived by the animal were also created by the animal, but this extraordinary sensory feat is carried out completely in the auditory medium. The information carrying capacity of the auditory sense in humans and other primates is much more limited. When you were trying to conjure up Scrooge's face, you were using your mind's eye, not your mind's ear. We can certainly make some judgments about the type of an object or animal and its approximate location by the sounds that it makes, but to understand the difference between the human senses of sight and hearing, we need only contrast the relative ease of mobility of deaf people and blind people. Who is more at risk walking near a cliff on a still day, a deaf person or a blind person?

If our sense of hearing is so inferior as an information-gathering device, why do we use it to support what is undeniably our most important communication and information-gathering system—language? Why should this be so when we consider that language may be the hallmark of our humanity? Let's consider what makes this possible—cross-modal sensory association or transfer in humans. This form of association in nonhuman primates seems to require reinforcement to make the link; that is, these animals may lack voluntary control over this sort of multisensory conceptual integration. The ability to abstract out a mental construct that involves a variety of sensory input allows us to attach arbitrary or conventional signs to these concepts, and it may have been one of the key human adaptations enabling speech. Why did speech become so dominant? Many commonsense explanations have been suggested: It works much better in the dark, it frees the hands for carrying objects and making tools, it may be more energy efficient, it does not require directed visual attention, etc. We need not dwell on these here—the point is that speech did become the dominant mode of communication for all hearing human societies.

If we think of a disability as something that reduces a person's capacity to function within a certain domain of behavior, then we might not classify blindness and deafness as sensory disabilities. Instead, we might say that blindness is primarily a mobility impairment and that deafness is a communication (but not language) disability. While we can readily understand this difference between the blind and the deaf, it is important to note that it is firmly rooted in the evolutionary history of the primates. The higher primates evolved as arboreal creatures that traveled rapidly from tree to tree through forest habitats by leaping and grasping limbs with their hands and feet. Vision was their master sense, and their hands and feet had to remain generalized, for grasping and manipulating objects, as well as for locomotion. Again, it is hard to imagine a blind arboreal monkey surviving past infancy, but all human societies include blind adults. One contributing factor is that blind people do not suffer from an inability to communicate their special needs through speech. Blind people might in some situations be seen as having special functions—as in the case of the probably legendary Homer, as a keeper of the oral (auditory) tradition.

On the other hand, the primary difficulty experienced by deaf people is precisely in the realm of communication, and in this regard we will consider the circumstances under which visible/gestural languages may develop and spread. This book argues that a central part of the human adaptation is intensive development of the higher primate capacity for successful group action, which, of course depends ultimately on the ability to communicate effectively. This book is not about the visible gestures that ordinarily and spontaneously accompany informal speech in all known human societies—instead it is about what is known of the history of visible gestures, especially those involving the hands, and signs that serve functions distinct from speech (although this distinction cannot always be precisely maintained, and we will occasionally stray into the former realm of discourse for illustrative purposes).

What Is Language?

This book uses a utilitarian definition of language. All human societies so far identified on Earth have languages, and if the users are not deaf, their primary language will be spoken. If they are deaf and are left unmolested by educators, physicians, and linguists, their primary language will be signed. We can take it as axiomatic, therefore, that all human beings have the capacity to develop and acquire languages in media that are accessible to their operating senses and musculoskeletal output systems. If we find a sign system operating as the primary mode of communication for a definable social group, we can conclude that it is a language. Sign systems used as secondary modes of communication, as are some encountered in this book, may be more problematic in this regard. Language scholars have, in the past, developed checklists of essential attributes of languages—for example the design features enumerated by Charles Hockett in 1960. This book avoids detailed formal definitions but includes for consideration and examination sign systems that appear capable of supporting the weight of most ordinary human interactions.

This work assumes that a continuum of linguistic complexity of manual gesture exists, from isolated gestures accompanying speech to full-fledged visible languages expressed fully in the sign languages of deaf communities. This capacity for linguistic elaboration is always there to be tapped, when needed or desired, in all human populations. The existence of this continuum presupposes fundamental processes whereby originally transparent or iconic signs become increasingly opaque or arbitrary through conventionalization or ritualization. Adam Kendon suggests that what is involved is not a simple one-dimensional continuum from more iconic to more conventionalized, however. Simple but conventionalized gestures that accompany speech may be more or less iconic, or not iconic at all. With respect to the latter point, Kendon (2004, 106) discusses the so-called "ring" hand, in sign language notation the 'F' hand. This is generally used to express approbation for a point made in conversation or for "perfection"—it is widely understood, and therefore conventionalized, but it

Fig. 4. The "F" handshape. Illustration by Robert C. Johnson.

does not appear iconic in any obvious way. The hands can be used to signify or denote a huge variety of concepts, and the shapes that do the signifying are subject to complex processes of conventionalization through use. The central argument being advanced, however, is that the potential for direct iconic representation by the hands provides the great wellspring for the emergence of new signs and, ultimately, the emergence of new human languages.

Before leaving this topic, however, it is worth considering an argument that suggests that the "ring" hand, OK gesture, or 'F' hand—however designated—may, in fact, have iconic roots deep in the evolutionary history of the human lineage (see figure 4). As the eminent anatomist and evolutionary anthropologist, John Napier, wrote:

> In man, the most precise function that the hand is capable of is to place the tip of the thumb in *opposition* to the tip of the index finger so that the pulps of the two digits make maximum contact. In this position, small objects can be manipulated with an unlimited potential for fine pressure adjustments or minute directional corrections. Opposition, to this degree of precision, is a hallmark of mankind. No nonhuman primate can replicate it. Although most people are unaware of the

> evolutionary symbolism of this finger-thumb opposition they
> cannot be unaware of its implication in international sign lan-
> guage; it is the universal gesture of human success. (1970, 181)

Napier does not suggest a distinct dividing line between the
gestural and the linguistic, between nonlanguage and language.
However, growth in the complexity of a gestural system entails the emergence of a conventionalized and componential
substructure (phonology), rules for combining these elements
(morphology), and methods for expressing relations among
actions and objects (syntax). The emergence of these structures can be directly observed in the processes by which sign
languages develop.

With regard to this functional approach to distinguishing
linguistically organized from nonlinguistic gesture, it is important to understand recent developments in the discipline of
linguistics, especially the controversies that have surrounded
the elaboration of the nativist or generative school of linguistics founded by Noam Chomsky in the 1950s. These developments can be contrasted with an older, anthropological
approach to linguistics and more recent progress in what has
come to be called cognitive linguistics. At the heart of this
controversy is the question of whether the human ability to
construct and use languages is a genetically determined special
trait or whether it emerges as a result of the application of
more general cognitive abilities to the need to communicate
about complex topics within social groups. Much about the
regularity of the organization of spoken languages suggests a
specific genetic determination. The well-known linguist and
writer, Steven Pinker, summarizes this evidence as follows:

> Chomsky's claim that from a Martian's-eye view all humans
> speak a single language is based on the discovery that the same
> symbol-manipulating machinery, without exception, underlies

the world's languages. Linguists have long known that the basic design features of language are found everywhere. Many were documented in 1960 by the non-Chomskyan linguist C. F. Hockett in a comparison between human languages and animal communication systems (Hockett was not acquainted with Martian). Languages use the mouth-to-ear channel as long as the users have intact hearing (manual and facial gestures, of course, are the substitute channel used by the deaf). A common grammatical code, neutral between production and comprehension, allows speakers to produce any linguistic message they can understand, and vice versa. Words have stable meanings, linked to them by arbitrary conventions. Speech sounds are treated discontinuously; a sound that is acoustically halfway between *bat* and *pat* does not mean something halfway between batting and patting. Languages can convey meanings that are abstract and remote in time or space from the speaker. Linguistic forms are infinite in number, because they are created by a discrete combinatorial system. Languages all show a duality of patterning in which one rule system is used to order phonemes within morphemes, independent of meaning, and another is used to order morphemes within words and phrases, specifying that meaning. (1994, 237–38)

It should be clear that sign languages might provide a test of the notion that languages are this rigorously constrained by genetic determination, in that, in contrast to spoken languages, they are organized within a completely different sensory medium, and they use a completely different set of musculoskeletal output systems. In fact, they have been used as evidence of both positions with respect to the biological foundation of the human capacity for language—specific genetic determination and general cognitive underpinnings. In this book, I will explore this question in some detail. According to linguists such as Pinker, there is language and not-language—there are no intermediate forms of communication or gradations between gesture and language. This book will argue that such gradations do exist and that gestural systems can become increasingly language-like through time and use. It will also be argued that, because of the fundamental iconicity of all sign languages, they do not have the sort of distinct duality of patterning that Pinker specifies as a hallmark of all languages. That is, on no level are the organizing principles of sign languages completely meaningless, as is true at the level of the phoneme in speech. For example, in sign languages big things are represented by big movements or spaces and small things are represented by small movements or spaces. Up means up and down means down, right means right and left means left, and so on. Nothing in speech compares to this. I also maintain categorically here that there is nothing primitive about this sort of organization—the sign languages of deaf people are complex and highly evolved, and they serve the same functions as the spoken languages of hearing people. It is just that they are transmitted and received in a different medium, and they take full advantage of that medium. As we will see, these languages have much to tell us about how to optimize communication in the visual medium, as our ability to exploit that medium expands exponentially through use of computers and the Internet.

With respect to their status as possible test cases, situations in which complex gestural or signing systems are known to have arisen include the following:

- In social groups that include a large proportion of deaf people;
- Among hearing people for use in situations where noise or distance impede vocal communication;
- Among hearing people for use as a *lingua franca;*
- Among hearing people who must be silent for religious or other reasons.

We will encounter examples of each of these cases, and this book will show what we can learn about the human capacity for language and communication by studying instances of human signing within a broad range of social contexts and geographic locations. A general goal will be to see what we can learn about the human condition in general by studying these exceptionally interesting examples of human behavior.

2 Signing Heritage

Signing in the Ancient World

Awareness of the sign languages of the deaf has a long history in the Western world. Plato famously has Socrates refer to the signing of deaf people in the dialogue *Cratylus:*

> *Socrates.* [H]ow do the primary names which precede analysis show the natures of things, as far as they can be shown; which they must do, if they are to be real names? . . . Suppose that we had no voice or tongue, and wanted to communicate with one another, should we not, like the deaf and dumb, make signs with the hands and head and the rest of the body?
>
> *Hermogenes.* There would be no choice, Socrates.
>
> *Soc.* We should imitate the nature of the thing; the elevation of our hands to heaven would mean lightness and upwardness; heaviness and downwardness would be expressed by letting them drop to the ground; the running of a horse, or any other animal, would be expressed by the most nearly similar gestures of our own frame. (Jowett, trans. 1901, 662)

Socrates's description of signing contains the essential point, appearing repeatedly in descriptions of the sign languages of the deaf throughout history, that these languages are somehow "natural, transparent, or iconic." This characteristic, depending on the historical context, may be seen as something positive or even noble, or as negative and primitive.

The Roman philosopher, Lucretius, was one of many to hypothesize that such gestural languages might have been the first languages (Aldrete 1999, 5). What is especially interesting is that these ancient thinkers could conceive of these gestural systems as forms of *language*. We also inherit from the ancient world a long tradition of meaningful gesture used by hearing people for a variety of purposes (see de Jorio 2002, 8).

On the subject of the expressiveness of these ancient gestural systems, Kendon quotes Quintilian, author of a great Roman treatise on oratory:

> As for the hands, without which all action would be crippled and enfeebled, it is scarcely possible to describe the variety of their motions, since they are almost as expressive as words. For other portions of the body merely help the speaker, whereas the hands may be almost said to speak. Do we not use them to demand, promise, summon, dismiss, threaten, supplicate, express aversion or fear, question or deny? Do we not employ them to indicate joy, sorrow, hesitation, confession, penitence, measure, quantity, number, and time? Have they not power to excite and prohibit, to express approval, wonder, or shame? Do they not take the place of adverbs and pronouns when we point at places and things? In fact, though the peoples and nations of the earth speak a multitude of tongues, they share in common the universal language of the hands. (2004, 18)

A connection of this tradition to the signing of deaf people is not remote. Because of the inherent limitations of communication by voice to large numbers of people before the invention of the electrically amplified microphone (Aldrete 1999, 75–76), public speaking in ancient Rome was almost always accompanied by conventionalized visible gesture (see figure 5). Aldrete points to the importance of public speaking as a significant part of the role expected of Roman patricians if they were to maintain their standing in the ancient city. In addition to the visual display of social position and demeanor through standardized gesture, these gestures were capable of conveying at least some of the meaning of the accompanying speech, when the speech itself could not be heard because

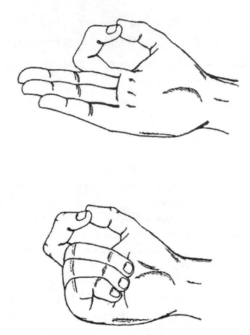

Fig. 5. Ancient Roman rhetorical gestures. From Gregory S Aldrete, *Gestures and Acclamations in Ancient Rome*, p. 39. figures 14 and 15. © 1999 The Johns Hopkins University Press. Reprinted with permission of The Johns Hopkins University Press.

of ambient noise or distance from the speaker. Roman orators also employed heralds who were placed at intervals away from the speaker and who were trained to repeat the orator's message, essentially to shout it to the assembled crowd. The problem of projection and audibility in public speaking continued into recent times. Even in the acoustically well-designed Cooper Union auditorium in New York, Abraham Lincoln felt the need to ask a friend to signal him visually from the back row if he was not audible at the beginning of the speech that launched his presidential candidacy in 1860 (Holzer 2004, 105).

Kendon also points to the "amplification" function of these rhetorical gestures in his discussion of the use of such gestures, inherited from the ancient Romans, in the noisy world of the nineteenth-century Neapolitan streets. Complex signing systems have also been reported in modern industrial settings where noise in the workplace makes spoken communication difficult or impossible (e.g., sawmills—Meissner and Philpott 1975). Later in this chapter, we will consider what is in many ways the opposite situation—where complex sign systems have emerged under conditions of enforced silence, especially in the monasteries of medieval Christian religious orders.

In the introduction to Kendon's translation of the classic nineteenth-century work, by the Italian priest Andrea de Jorio, detailing the use of the Neapolitan gestural system to overcome the noise and confusion of the nineteenth-century city, Kendon quotes a footnote from de Jorio:

> [T]he language of our low people is double, with words and gestures. This second is at once full of grace and philosophy. It is surprising to see two persons at a distance from one another and in the middle of the chaos of the more populated streets of Naples speak with one another and understand each other well. (de Jorio 2002, xlviii)

However, de Jorio will not go so far as to call this Neapolitan gestural system the equivalent of a second language:

> In case anyone thinks that this work also aims to show that gesture is a language, let us lay before him the following confession. We agree with the scientists in saying that gestural expression was not a language, and we emphasize this point so that when, in the course of this work, the expression 'gesture language' (*linguaggio mimico*) is encountered, it will be understood that it is not used in the strict sense . . . So far as the resemblance between gesturing and spoken eloquence (*loquela*) is concerned, or even its superiority in some cases,

the reader is referred to the entire work, but in particular the titles that deal with the role of gesture in Rhetoric. (p. 8)

Although one might conclude that, in fact, he does much to establish at least the semilinguistic bona fides of Neapolitan gesture, he wishes to maintain the intellectual respectability of his central thesis, which, again, tries to establish a link between the nineteenth-century Neapolitan gestural system and ancient Roman rhetorical gesture.

The following charming description of the "mano cornuta" or horned hand, as pictured in figure 6, is given by de Jorio (in Garrick Mallery):

> This gesture . . . has many significations, according to the subject-matter and context, and also as applied to different parts of the body. Applied to the head it has allusion, descending from high antiquity, to a marital misfortune which was probably common in prehistoric times as well as the present. It is also often used as an amulet against the *jettatura* or evil eye, and misfortune in general, and directed toward another person is a prayerful wish for his or her preservation from evil. This use is ancient, as is shown on medals and statues, and is sup-

Fig. 6. Neapolitan woman employing the "mano cornuta" or horned hand in the course of an argument—the gesture is also portrayed in ancient Roman art. De Jorio reproduced in Mallery 1881.

posed by some to refer to the horns of animals slaughtered in sacrifice. The position of the fingers ... is also given as one of Quintilian's oratorical gestures by the words "*Duo quoque medii sub pollicem veniunt,*" and is said by him to be vehement and connected with reproach or argument. In the present case, as a response to an impertinent or disagreeable petition, it simply means, "instead of giving what you ask, I will give you nothing but what is vile and useless, as horns are." (Mallery 1881)

The process by which the "horned hand" comes to represent the cuckold, as de Jorio alludes to in his description ("marital misfortune"), provides some insight into the processes that underlie the creation of sign/referent linkages generally. Western culture contains pervasive symbolism, whereby a cuckold is mocked by making him wear horns or referring to him as having horns. So, a handshape that iconically represents horns comes to have, through a metaphorical process, "cuckold" as one of its meanings. Fans of American college football will, of course, recognize the sign as emblematic of the University of Texas "Longhorns."

If a link between classical Roman gestures and the gestures of the nineteenth-century Neapolitan streets can indeed be established, as de Jorio argues persuasively, it suggests considerable stability of these gestures over time, further reinforcing the notion of their similarity to linguistic words and signs. In other words, they appear to be much more than simple ad hoc gestures, made up on the spot, for very limited purposes.

In addition to its use to amplify public rhetorical presentations, another significant factor in the original elaboration of this ancient Italic gestural system was the polyglot situation that developed in Rome as the republic and then the empire expanded. Aldrete describes the elaborate development of pantomime and pantomime dance during this period, although the anecdote he describes may be apocryphal:

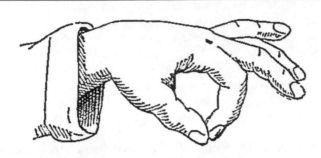

Fig. shows the extremities of the index and thumb closely joined in form of a cone, and turned down, the other fingers held at pleasure, and the hand and arm advanced to the point and held steady. This signifies *justice*, a just person, that which is just and right. The same sign may denote friendship, a menace, which specifically is that of being brought to justice, and snuff, *i.e.* powdered tobacco; but the expression of the countenance and the circumstance of the use of the sign determine these distinctions. Its origin is clearly the balance or emblem of justice, the office of which consists in ascertaining physical weight, and thence comes the moral idea of distinguishing clearly what is just and accurate and what is not. The hand is presented in the usual manner of holding the balance to weigh articles.

Fig. 7. Illustration of a Neapolitan gesture from DeJorio, the "ring" or "F" hand. Reprinted from Mallery 1881.

A popular anecdote involving pantomime dancers concerned a Pontic ruler who visited Rome during the reign of Nero and witnessed such a show. Although he could not understand the words of the songs and speeches accompanying the dance, he was able to follow the performance and understood everything by watching the gestures of the dancers. Astonished by this, the king asked Nero to let him take one of the pantomimes back to his kingdom in the belief that the dancer's gestures were so eloquent that he would be able to dispose of his interpreters and use the dancer to communicate with his linguistically varied neighbors. (1999, 51–53)

There appears to be a direct connection between these elaborate gestural systems and the modern sign languages of the deaf through the sign systems developed by Christian religious orders (see figure 8). Aldrete (1999, 73) also notes the attention given to gesture in the writings of prominent ecclesiastical figures, including Augustine.

Monastic Signing Systems

During the medieval period, European monastic communities that placed high spiritual value on silence developed systems of communication by manual signs. This tradition is of particular significance because the first documented attempts to educate deaf children through manual communication were carried out by Pedro Ponce de Leon, a Spanish Benedictine monk whose efforts appear to have been influenced by knowledge of monastic sign systems (Plann 1993; Bruce 2007). A good deal is known about such sign systems from historical sources and from their survival into modern times in Trappist (strictly observant Cistercian) monasteries.

In the early 1970s, Robert Barakat conducted research on the Cistercian sign language in use at an abbey in Massachusetts. According to the *Regulations of the Order of Cistercians of the Strict Observance* (1975):

> In making the signs, the right hand is always used when only one hand is necessary; and when one finger is sufficient, the forefinger is always used, unless another is specifically mentioned. Noises with the mouth in order to make the signs understood are absolutely forbidden.

Barakat notes that this restriction is also true for unofficial signs and that the monks of this abbey employed a signed alphabet for fingerspelling words.

Fig. 8. Benedictine gesture. Zurbaran, Francisco de (1598–1664). Saint Benedict. Oil on canvas, 74 × 40 3/4 in. (188 × 103.5 cm). Bequest of Harry G. Sperling, 1971 (1976.100.21). Image copyright © The Metropolitan Museum of Art / Art Resource, NY. Image Reference: ART377358.

Barakat provides detailed descriptions of the signs in use at the abbey, and some of the flavor of their construction is conveyed in this discussion of how ambiguity may be introduced into signed conversation, as well as how it is avoided when the context for use of a particular sign is clear:

> [W]hen a third conversational participant, or even a fourth, is added to those signing, the angle of vision presents a definite problem. For example the sign for TYPEWRITER requires that the signer extend his hands before him, and move them up and down as though typing on a machine. However, the sign, on occasions observed at St. Joseph's, has been misinterpreted as PLAY or PIANO simply because these too require that the hands be outstretched before the body but moved on a level plane without any up and down motion. When these signs are made in a face-to-face interaction between two signers, as is most commonly the case, they are easily differentiated, if made correctly.

Development of Sign-Based Education of the Deaf

The development of sophisticated educational methods for deaf students was roughly contemporaneous with the period of intellectual ferment in Western Europe, especially France—generally known as the Enlightenment—during the mid-seventeenth to the late eighteenth century. Characteristics of the Enlightenment that appeal to a modern audience are its emphasis on the power of human reason over superstition, the emergence of modern science, and the idea that human beings could be "perfected" through appropriate education; the eighteenth-century French philosopher Jean-Jacques Rousseau being perhaps the leading proponent of the latter view (see *Emile, où de l'éducation*). An additional essential element of the Enlightenment was the idea of liberation—liberating the individual from the effects of religious dogma or political oppression. There seems to be little doubt that these notions ultimately influenced the development of deaf education, but the earliest known systematic use of sign language to educate deaf children formally appears to have had, at least in part, a religious motivation as well as a liberating function, at least from a Christian perspective: liberation from sin and from ignorance of God.

As mentioned earlier, Pedro Ponce de Leon, a Spanish Benedictine monk, carried out the earliest recorded attempt of this kind. However, the tradition that is of most interest here began with a French priest, the Abbé Charles-Michel de l'Epée in the mid-eighteenth century. Epée founded the national school for the deaf in Paris, and he is generally credited with initiating the movement that led to the founding of schools for the deaf, based in instruction in sign language, throughout Europe and the Americas. If we see deaf communities as functioning as linguistic or even ethnic groups, and we acknowledge that all known social groups have stories or myths concerning their founding, it is not surprising that the story of Epée's discovery of two deaf girls takes on the mantle of an origin myth for the signing deaf community of France and, eventually, the United States as well. In their book, *Deaf in America,* Padden and Humphries report on having seen the following signed recitation of the story at a deaf club in Marseilles:

> The Abbé de l'Epée had been walking for a long time through a dark night. He wanted to stop and rest overnight, but he could not find a place to stay, until at a distance he saw a house with a light. He stopped at the house, knocked at the door, but no one answered. He saw that the door was open, so he entered the house and found two young women seated by the fire sewing. He spoke to them, but still they did not respond. He walked closer and spoke to them again, but they failed again to respond. The Abbé was perplexed, but seated himself beside them. They looked up at him but did

not speak. At that point, their mother entered the room. Did the Abbé not know that her daughters were deaf? He did not, but now he understood why they had not responded. As he contemplated the young women, the Abbé realized his vocation. (1988, 7)

The storyteller goes on to assert a key additional part of the myth—that it was the Abbé who went on to invent their beautiful sign language. Padden and Humphries point out that the Abbé himself did not necessarily make this claim, and instead the Abbé suggests that such languages may arise spontaneously among deaf people themselves:

Every deaf-mute sent to us already has a language. He is thoroughly in the habit of using it, and understands others who do. With it he expresses his needs, desires, pains, and so on, and makes no mistake when others express themselves likewise. (p. 28)

Perhaps Harlan Lane in his monumental *When the Mind Hears* (1984) gives the best-known detailed account of this origin myth. Lane tells much of this story in the persona of Laurent Clerc, the deaf French teacher who was brought to the United States by T. H. Gallaudet to found the first permanent school for the deaf in the United States at Hartford in 1817— it thus becomes the origin myth for the American signing deaf community as well. The source of the title for Lane's book is worth mentioning here, as it expresses with unusual poignancy the feelings many deaf people have for the revelation that is their first encounter with sign language and its role in opening their minds to understanding the world around them. The quotation is attributed to Victor Hugo and is directed to Ferdinand Berthier, the great deaf teacher of the deaf: "What matters deafness of the ear, when the mind hears? The one true deafness, the incurable deafness, is that of the mind."

Where religion is a matter of adoption of a belief system, as much as ritualized practice, this opening of the mind becomes all important. This principle at work can be seen among Protestants as well as the Catholic clerics described so far. Carty, Macready, and Sayers (2009) discuss the case of Sarah Pratt, a deaf woman in early Massachusetts. In the Puritan practice of religion, "conversion" was extremely important, conversion implying "an inward event—a profound experience of God—rather than public adherence to a particular system of belief (p. 296)." Demonstration of conversion required examination by church elders, and the great Puritan preacher, Increase Mather, documented Sarah's conversion. According to Mather, Sarah acquired the knowledge necessary for her conversion through both signs and a level of English literacy she had somehow acquired.

There is little question that this was part of the motivation for T. H. Gallaudet, a Protestant minister, in bringing Clerc back with him from France. From a religious perspective, it may make little difference that instruction is through the medium of sign, as opposed to speech—the goal is to make the "word" of God accessible. As we will see, the medium itself becomes the message later on in the context of Victorian progressivism, when oral education and "returning the deaf person to hearing society" becomes the goal and the mantra.

Sophia Rosenfeld (2001, 13–56) argues that French Enlightenment and revolutionary thinkers saw sign language as "natural," uncorrupted by uses for political oppression, and they were familiar with Epée's program to educate deaf children using sign language. The supposed naturalness of signed language is a recurring theme in Western thought—that it is somehow more "natural" than spoken language. Eventually this argument gets extended to visually based, concrete, iconic language in general—see the discussion of Ezra Pound's work in the last chapter—direct, visually based language is seen as having the potential to free the mind from obfuscation and unnecessary complexity. Part of the Enlightenment program, that of seeking materialistic or scientific explanations of human origins that had once been entirely the province of religion, found expression in the emergence of theories about the origin of language. Thinking in this realm intersected with interest in the education of the deaf and the use of sign language. The Abbé de Condillac, a leading French eighteenth-century *philosophe,* was heavily involved in the redeployment of considerations of language origins in gesture that first appear in classical antiquity.

The earliest information that comes close to providing a linguistic description of a natural sign language has to do with French Sign Language (Langue des Signes Française or LSF). LSF is frequently said to have originated with the founding of the school for the deaf by the Abbé de l'Epée in Paris during the mid-eighteenth century. It appears likely, however, that Epée drew on an existing sign language in formulating his system of "methodical" signs that were intended to support instruction in the written French language and that were grammatically modeled on that language. We have seen that there may have been some influence from the monastic tradition of signing, but it is also possible that there were sign systems already in use by some of the deaf students who came to his school. Little is known about natural sign languages that might have been in use by the French deaf community either before or immediately after the founding of Epée's school, but what appears to be the first book ever published by a deaf author, Pierre Desloges's 1779 *Observations of a Deaf-Mute* is one source. Desloges made it clear in his book that grammatical differences between the French language and the sign language used by deaf people existed, especially with respect to the use of space, including the use of directional signs (Fischer 2002).

Desloges also proposed a taxonomy of LSF signs. According to Fischer, Desloges maintained that there are three classes of signs: ordinary or primitive signs, reflected signs, and analytic signs. As described, these are fairly familiar categories: The first comprises "natural signs which all peoples of the world, hearing or deaf, use frequently"—these are the largely iconic gestures of ordinary discourse that are incorporated into the sign language. The second category of signs "can also be described as natural, but which can only be produced and understood with a certain amount of reflection." Finally, analytic signs stand "for concepts which are not suited for direct, pictorial expression." Desloges, thus, categorized the signs of this early form of LSF in terms of their relative iconicity (Fischer 2002).

While the historical route whereby LSF came to influence the development of American Sign Language (ASL) is well known to the American deaf community, it is worth recounting. This influence began with the arrival of Laurent Clerc in the United States to begin his partnership with Thomas Hopkins Gallaudet at the American School for the Deaf in Hartford in the early nineteenth century. Gallaudet brought Clerc, a deaf teacher, from France to begin the practice of teaching deaf children in sign language. Certainly, Clerc would at first have been teaching in LSF, but eventually a new language began to emerge, almost certainly incorporating elements of existing American sign systems, probably including the sign language of Martha's Vineyard (to be discussed in the next chapter). Commenting on the belief of Jean Marc Itard,

a ninteenth-century physician and teacher at the Paris school
for the deaf, that LSF was highly iconic, Lane outlines some
of the processes that might have been at work, assuming, as
many linguists, do that modern ASL is much less iconic:

> Perhaps . . . Franslan [LSF] was more iconic than Ameslan
> [ASL]. There are two reasons for thinking this. First, as signs
> are handed down from generation to generation, as the pri-
> mary language of the family, from parent to child who be-
> comes a parent in turn, they become simpler, more regular;
> they are shaped by the general rules for sign formation and
> thus become more encoded. Second, Franslan built originally
> on family signs brought to it by children like Massieu and
> his predecessors under Epée. De Gérando tells us that these
> children from isolated parts of France often brought similar
> signs for the same things. (1976, 235–36)

ASL is the sign language that has been most thoroughly described and analyzed in linguistic terms, and this passage from
Lane reflects a theoretical position that developed during the
1960s and 1970s to explain the obvious iconicity of ASL but
nevertheless preserve its linguistic status. Early theory assumed
that, while elements of the language might initially be introduced iconically, most iconicity was squeezed out over time by
purely linguistic processes (Frishberg 1975; Klima and Bellugi
1979). Sherman Wilcox has referred to this tendency among
linguists as an attempt to banish the "specter" of iconicity (see
Armstrong and Wilcox 2007, 77–80), assumed to be necessary
if the presumption is accepted that linguistic signs must be
arbitrary. However, there are now linguistically sophisticated
approaches to the description of ASL that assume the iconicity
is not only involved at the beginnings of sign formation but
that it is also basic to the ongoing grammatical processes of
sign languages (Taub 2001; P. Wilcox 2000).

Signing deaf communities sprang up in the many residential schools for the deaf that were established in Europe and the Americas during the early to mid-nineteenth century, following the model created by the Abbé de l'Epée (for an account of these developments in the United States, see Van Cleve and Crouch 1989; for France, see Delaporte 2002). These flourishing communities were dealt a severe blow during the latter part of the century, especially following the international congress of educators of the deaf held in Milan in 1880. This congress voted to support oral-only education of the deaf, involving speechreading and vocal training, and to suppress sign-based education. Some of these signing communities are recovering only now and only to be threatened by new

Fig. 9. Thomas Hopkins Gallaudet (left), for whom Gallaudet University is named. His name sign, and the sign for Gallaudet University (right), is made by indicating the temple piece of his spectacles. Image of T. H. Gallaudet courtesy of the Gallaudet University Archives. The sign illustration is reproduced from Clayton Valli, ed., *The Gallaudet Dictionary of American Sign Language*, p. 189. Washington, DC: Gallaudet University Press.

demographic trends and technological and genetic approaches to the treatment of deafness as a medical condition.

Gallaudet and a Signing Community in Higher Education

This chapter concludes with an historical sketch of the world's only higher education institution for deaf people—Gallaudet University—which from its inception has employed a sign language, what is now generally known as ASL, in the teaching and transmission of advanced knowledge. Gallaudet is, thus, a unique laboratory for observing how sign languages may evolve as the complexity of their subject matter increases and as they inevitably interact with the spoken languages of the majority scholarly community. Gallaudet University is also almost certainly the largest signing community gathered in one place on Earth, currently comprising about three thousand people, more than half of whom are deaf.

Gallaudet was established in the District of Columbia as a school for deaf and blind children by Amos Kendall, an American political figure, and Edward M. Gallaudet, son of Thomas H. Gallaudet. It became eligible for federal support in legislation signed by President Franklin Pierce in 1857 and has received annual funding from the U.S. Congress since 1858. The institution was authorized, by legislation signed by none other than Abraham Lincoln, to confer collegiate degrees in 1864, and it has been granting bachelor's degrees to deaf students since the late 1860s. From the beginning, its undergraduate program was designed to be like that of other American colleges, including within its organizational structure an independent faculty providing an essentially liberal arts curriculum, as well as student organizations, including some of the oldest intercollegiate athletic teams in the United

States. This combination of a broad spectrum of instructional programs and opportunities for leadership of student organizations has been integral to Gallaudet's role in preparing an educated leadership for the American deaf community, until recently making the American deaf community unique in this regard. Gallaudet has shared a similar role to that of the historically black colleges and universities (HBCUs) in the United States, but Gallaudet has been unique in providing this sort of environment for deaf students, while there have been many HBCUs.

People outside the deaf community find it difficult to understand the role Gallaudet plays in that community. Gallaudet was established as a private corporation even though it received federal support, and it has always been governed by a self-replacing board of trustees. As a result, it has been relatively free of government control over its curriculum and methods of instruction, and instruction has always involved sign language. Dirksen Bauman has written about what this has meant to the world deaf community:

> In order to understand . . . one has to appreciate the near mythic role that Gallaudet University plays within the Deaf world. It is the only plot of land in the entire world where Deaf people have direct access to higher education through a signed language. Historically, Gallaudet has been a bastion of signed-language instruction even during a time when all residential schools in the United States banned ASL. (2009, 93)

Gallaudet continues to be the only higher education institution in the world where, after entering the university's gate, a deaf student finds him or herself in a generally barrier-free communication environment. Deaf students have always had the opportunity to attend colleges and universities other than Gallaudet, and increasingly a broad array of support services have been offered, but Gallaudet remains the only university that offers this environment—this was Congress's intent in creating it, and deaf students continue to seek it from among the spectrum of other institutions open to them. It is highly unlikely that such an environment could ever be created elsewhere.

Gallaudet has provided a laboratory for study of the ways in which vernaculars develop into specialized registers for scholarly or technical use, and it allows for study of the ways in which signed languages may be influenced by the dominant spoken languages of their surrounding communities. Gallaudet has provided a safe haven for signed language use in education and advanced discourse during a time when its use for this purpose was all but eliminated elsewhere. It is possible to trace the course of its evolution for this purpose: from the early years through written descriptions, and, from the inception of motion picture technology in the late nineteenth century, by direct observation (see, e.g., Supalla 2004).

The languages used for academic discourse in universities throughout the world are specialized prestige registers, including substantial lexicons designed to provide for the needs of the fields of study they support. Much is known about the historical course that English followed as it evolved to serve scholarly and commercial purposes, and this process was analogous to what happened to the ASL used at Gallaudet during the past century and a half. While English is classified phylogenetically as a Germanic language, most of its lexicon is derived from other linguistic stocks, notably from Greek and Latin, but especially the latter. The influx of Latin lexicon into English occurred largely in several waves. Although Latin had begun to enter the English lexicon with the Christian conversion of the Anglo-Saxons, the Norman Conquest of

England led to the introduction of numerous French words that were ultimately derived from Latin. Another major wave is perhaps of more interest here. This occurred generally during the seventeenth and eighteenth centuries as English began to replace Latin as the language of scientific and scholarly purposes in the English-speaking world.

While the signed language used for instruction at Gallaudet has been built upon a vernacular ASL platform, it has, in turn, been heavily influenced by English. This occurred, at least in part, for much the same reason that academic Latin terminology was hauled bodily into the English language register used at English speaking universities during the seventeenth and eighteenth centuries—there was a need for specialized words and no reason not to use the resources that were already at hand. Motion pictures from the turn of the twentieth century make it clear that English was incorporated into the learned discourse of deaf people at this time primarily through the medium of fingerspelling. Fingerspelling made the entire lexicon of English potentially available for use as needed by literate ASL signers (in this regard, see the special issue of *Sign Language Studies,* 2004, vol. 4, no. 3, devoted to research on the so-called NAD [National Association of the Deaf] and Gallaudet films), and fingerspelling was used liberally at this time. Carol Padden has analyzed the well-known 1913 film of George Veditz, entitled *The Preservation of the Sign Language* (Padden 2004). She concludes that his extensive use of fingerspelling, including entire fingerspelled sentences, may have been partly to demonstrate to oralist critics of sign language that deaf people could become entirely literate in English, even while communicating primarily in ASL. Over time, there has been a transition at Gallaudet to a situation in which the use of fingerspelling seems to have decreased, to be replaced by the mouthing of English words, in association with ASL signs, to disambiguate an underlying English message. Padden (2004, 256) points out that Veditz, like other deaf people at the time, strongly disapproved of the use of lip movements and speech while signing.

The practice currently evolving at Gallaudet must be distinguished from two other methods of introducing English into signed utterances that have been widely used in the education of deaf children during the latter half of the twentieth century—Signed English and what has been called Simultaneous Communication (SimCom). Signed English most closely resembles the methodical signs used in France in the late eighteenth and early nineteenth centuries—the goal was to use natural and invented signs to represent essentially all, or at least most, of the English morphemes visibly in the course of a signed utterance. SimCom, on the other hand, involves an attempt to speak an English sentence more or less normally while simultaneously producing a sign stream that is supposed to represent the spoken English, more or less completely. The practice currently in use at Gallaudet has been influenced by these two practices—however, it is identical to neither, either in underlying philosophy or actual practice. This form of signing, over time, has been influenced in a direction away from either SimCom or signed English by two major forces: At least when used by hearing people, speech has become suppressed to be replaced by selective mouthing of words; and many of the spatial aspects of ASL signing are incorporated into the sign stream. At the risk of employing an anachronism, it is also clear that some sort of continuum exists among the signers on the Gallaudet campus along an ASL-English axis. One interesting phenomenon is that whether or not an individual is deaf is not a reliable predictor of his or her placement on this axis.

This does not mean that fingerspelling is no longer employed to introduce English elements into ASL. Initialization is a particularly important device, whereby the first letter of an English word may be used in the formation of a sign or an English word may be abbreviated as in "AC" for air conditioning to create an ASL sign that precisely denotes the English term. Another practice that has been used extensively is to sign a word or phrase, then fingerspell its English translation, then, when it is signed again, its English equivalent can be assumed.

This evolutionary process in the development of ASL as an academic language should not be taken to mean that there has not been controversy surrounding the roles of deaf people and sign language on the university's campus. In 1988, Gallaudet students and graduates organized a protest to demand the appointment of the first deaf president in the university's 120 year history, following the appointment of a hearing person to that position. The movement they created, known as Deaf President Now or DPN, succeeded; and a deaf president was appointed by the university's board of trustees. Since that time, Gallaudet has been governed by a majority deaf board and an administration managed by deaf people. No other higher education institution in the world exists where deaf students can interact with policy makers and administrators, at the highest level, who are also deaf.

This change in the university's governance, however, did not end all dissension on the campus. Protest erupted again in 2006 when a now deaf-majority board appointed a deaf woman to succeed the first deaf president, following his retirement. Once again, the protests forced a change in the appointment, the woman who had been appointed was removed, and a different deaf person was installed as president. There is no question that the causes of this protest were complex, certainly involving personal and group politics. However, some fundamental issues have been identified. John Christiansen, a member of the original presidential search committee, comments as follows:

> I suggest that part of the explanation is that Gallaudet University is more than just a university. The ninety-nine-acre, fenced-in campus is in some ways closer to Vatican City than is our counterpart in Northeast DC, the Catholic University of America. In many ways, we on the search committee were not so much in the business of selecting a new university president as choosing a new "pope." (2009, 85)

The university's position on language, particularly sign language, and more particularly ASL, came under much scrutiny during and after the protest. Especially important in this discussion has been the extent to which the ASL used in the classrooms at Gallaudet should be influenced by the grammatical structures of the English language. While this remains an unresolved issue in many ways, the Gallaudet board, for the first time, adopted a new statement that explicitly recognizes the bilingual, English/ASL, mission of the institution.

In addition, Christiansen identifies, as one of the causes of the protest, anxiety about the future of the deaf community in general.

> Perhaps another part of the explanation of the mass reaction in 2006 is that many Deaf people have become quite concerned about the future of their community. This concern, which has probably increased since DPN, may help explain why there was perhaps even more anger and emotion in 2006 than in 1988. For example, the number of students in residential schools for deaf students is much lower than it was a few

decades ago. According to the Gallaudet Research Institute's
Annual Survey of Deaf and Hard of Hearing Children and
Youth, which monitors this on an annual basis, only about 25
percent of deaf and hard-of-hearing students are now educated in these traditional breeding grounds of Deaf culture
(compared to approximately 55 percent who were educated
either in residential schools or in day schools for deaf students
in the mid-1970s). Many more deaf students today are in some
type of mainstreamed educational setting. One consequence
of this transformation is that Gallaudet University is now the
primary agent of socialization for many people into the Deaf
community. In addition, approximately eighty thousand children around the world, primarily in wealthy nations, have
received cochlear implants. Many people in Deaf communities
in the United States and abroad are worried about what will
happen as a consequence of this technological development.
Many of these children, particularly the increasing number
who are receiving implants at a very young age (including
a rapidly increasing number who are receiving bilateral implants), are not likely to be a part of a signing Deaf community
in the future. (2009, 85–86)

Commenting on the significance of the 1988 DPN movement and the demographic and technological trends threat-
ening a cohesive deaf community, Van Cleve and Crouch,
writing in 1989 struck a hopeful note concerning the future
of the deaf community, especially, it is argued in the current
book, the signing community that Gallaudet represents:

Still the future of the deaf community is not bleak. Its history has shown that deaf people realize that in community
they have strength. If they understand that history and heed
its lessons, they will be able to unite to define their interests
again and to preserve their victories, refashioning their objec-
tives and their methods to meet the new conditions of the
twentieth and twenty-first centuries. One indication that they
will do so was the Deaf President Now strike that paralyzed
Gallaudet University in the spring of 1988 and brought about
a revolution in that venerable institution's leadership. (p. 171)

The next chapter explores instances in which sign languages appear to have arisen spontaneously, without input or direction from educators. These cases include social groups with large or small numbers of deaf people—or no deaf people at all. Researchers are starting to understand the process by which these languages emerge, and there is overwhelming evidence for a universal human capacity to create such languages under the appropriate circumstances.

3   Signing Communities

SIGN LANGUAGES DEVELOP when local populations include substantial numbers of deaf people, and these languages may be used extensively by the hearing people in these communities as well as the deaf people. Knowledge is also accumulating about the course of development these emerging languages generally follow.

Signing Deaf Communities

A brief review of some of the known cases where sign languages, or at least sophisticated sign systems have arisen, apparently spontaneously, provides a good place to start the discussion. Perhaps the best-known example is that of the signing community that apparently existed on the Massachusetts island of Martha's Vineyard during the eighteenth and nineteenth centuries. Because of a genetic founder effect and a high rate of inbreeding on the island, a high frequency of genetic deafness existed in the population. Apparently, the sign language came into frequent use by the hearing islanders as well as by their deaf relatives and neighbors. Similar situations have been documented in other small-scale traditional societies, notably in Central America and Bali. It has been claimed that the Vineyard sign language was one of the bases, along with the French Sign Language introduced in the United States by Laurent Clerc and T. H. Gallaudet, for the subsequent development of ASL at the American School for the Deaf in Hartford, Connecticut, a school attended by many Vineyard islanders during the nineteenth century. This story of the contributions to the development of a sign language, in a national or local school for the deaf, from both indigenous and educational sources may be typical of what happened throughout Europe and the Americas during the ninteenth century.

Groce's quotation of testimony by an elderly man in the late twentieth century provides a sense of the sociolinguistic situation on the island, long after the signing deaf community had disappeared:

> We would sit around and wait for the mail to come in and just talk. And the deaf would be there, everyone would be there. And they were just part of the crowd, and they were accepted. They were fishermen and farmers and everything else. And they wanted to find out the news, just as much as the rest of us. And oftentimes people would tell stories and make signs at the same time so everyone could follow him together. Of course, sometimes, if there were more deaf than hearing there, everyone would speak sign language—just to be polite you know. (1985, 60)

Branson, Miller, and Masaja describe a similar situation on the Indonesian island of Bali:

> This article introduces the people and sign language of a very special village in north Bali, in eastern Indonesia. Like the community of Martha's Vineyard, this village has a substantial hereditary Deaf population that uses sign language, a language known and used freely by hearing members of the village. Unlike the sign language of Martha's Vineyard, the sign language of this Balinese village has emerged within the confines of the village. Most importantly, the population and the language are alive and well. (1996, 39)

Erich Fox Tree has recently documented a well-developed sign language complex, or group of related sign languages

(Meemul Tziij), among deaf populations of Maya in Meso-america. (Originally described by Robert E. Johnson in 1992.) He suggests that this complex has ancient roots, and he documents what appears to be precursors of current signs depicted in ancient Maya art and iconography (see figure 10):

> Scholars have long asserted that the gestures depicted in Classic Maya iconography look like representations of some ancient sign language, and epigraphers have come to accept numerous relationships between hand-shaped Maya hiero-glyphs and conventionalized gestures used by hearing Mayas today . . . only a few have acknowledged the existence of contemporary living sign languages. . . . Nonetheless, parallels between ancient iconography and modern signs deserve attention, such as cases of ancient figures that appear to sign concepts related to their own identities. (2009, 353)

Fox Tree makes a convincing case for the ancient roots and longevity of well-developed and related sign languages distributed across a wide area of Mesoamerica, and he concludes by illuminating concisely much about what has been discussed so far:

> Why has Meemul Tziij persisted so long, and why have certain signs remained so stable? One factor is the persistence of local Deaf communities in places with higher-than-normal incidences of congenital deafness and in the societally bilingual village of Chican in communities with lower (but still notable) rates of bimodal bilingualism, such as Nahualá. Yet the example of Plains Sign Talk [PST] in North America [see below] suggests that the persistence of isolated deaf populations is not the only factor; while the Native nations in which PST has persisted most strongly are ones with (deaf and hearing) populations formerly reputed to be the most proficient in PST, they are also the ones with populations that have strong social rituals that involve PST. . . . Continued use of Meemul Tziij as a supplemental language by elders, as one of several linguae francae by merchants, and as an alternate language

A: Basic handshape for MILPA ("maize-plant[s]" or "maize field"), employing the CL:PLANT orientation/handshape.

B: Nahualeño signing MILPA holding the right hand outward. The sign connotes the height and draping leaves of an imaginary (healthy) maize plant.

C: MILPA in Yucatán. The signer traces the stalk and leaves of an invisible maize plant. This sign does not seem to be used outside of the Yucatán Peninsula.

D: The Maize God signs MILPA while seated in an image on a Classic-Period "Tikal Dancer Plate" (after Kerr photograph #3933, © Justin Kerr).

E: The Maize God signs MILPA with his right hand while dancing on another "Tikal dancer plate" (after photograph #5258, © Justin Kerr). The left hand recalls a sign for MAIZE-EAR still employed in Chiapas.

F: The sign for MAIZE-EAR in Chiapas is nearly identical to the sign for INFANT (literally, "very small person") used in Chiapas and Western Guatemala (including in Nahualá). The similarity likely reflects the widespread folk belief maize plants cradle maize-ears like mothers cradle infants. Cognate signs are found elsewhere across Mesoamerica sharing a similar folk belief. (For instance, Nahualeños use an identical sign for INFANT, while their sign for MAIZE-EAR is similar, except that both hands are clenched in fists.)

Fig. 10. Contemporary Mayan signs and Classic Maya epigraphy. From Fox Tree 2009. Images © Erich Fox Tree.

by people with ritual or practical need for silence hints at the enduring utility of sign languages across Mesoamerica. (2009, 357)

An additional case that merits discussion is that of the Caribbean island of Providence described by William Washabaugh (1986). In this case, about twenty deaf islanders lived among a total population of 3,000 in the 1970s at the time of the study. Washabaugh (p. 27) describes the language as being highly iconic, indexic, and context dependent. With respect to its use by the island population generally, he comments:

> Deaf islanders today sign in the fashion of their predecessors going back at least three generations into the past. And, in some villages, the preceding generations of deaf persons have been available to provide signing input to subsequent generations. The hearing promote the use of signing among the deaf. Hearing islanders would not think of communicating with the deaf in any way other than by signing. (p. 9)

In order to round out the emerging picture of geographic and ethnic diversity, there are two recently described situations involving a Bedouin community in Israel and the emergence of a sign language within the deaf education system of Nicaragua. The latter case, it should be noted, does not represent a language used by a small community of deaf and hearing signers, but it does illustrate some of the features of the process by which a new sign language emerges.

A popular book by Margalit Fox (2007; and see Sandler et al. 2005) describes the Bedouin case. The Bedouin community occupies a settled village in Israel and is not nomadic. The sign language used in the village appears to be unique—it is distinct from the sign language used by other Israeli deaf people and in Israeli schools and programs for the deaf. Fox describes the language and the community that uses it:

> The language is Al-Sayyid's genetic legacy. In this isolated
> traditional community, where marriage to outsiders is rare, a
> form of inherited deafness has been passed down from one
> generation to the next for the last 70 years. Of the 3,500
> residents of the village today, nearly 150 are deaf, an inci-
> dence forty times that of the general population. As a result,
> an indigenous signed language has sprung up here, evolving
> among the deaf villagers as a means of communication. That
> can happen whenever deaf people come together. But what is
> so striking about the sign language of Al-Sayyid is that many
> hearing villagers can also speak it. It permeates every aspect
> of community life here, used between parents and children,
> husbands and wives, from sibling to sibling and neighbor to
> neighbor. At every hour of the day, in the houses, in the fields
> and in the mosque, there are people conversing in sign. (p. 7)

Often these situations share a few common features: the societies are small in scale, so that most of the individuals involved
know each other or may even be related in some way; the
frequency of deafness is relatively high; and deaf and hearing
people are in fairly constant interaction with one another.
Finally, because of the factors of relatedness and interdepen-
dence in such societies, the hearing members are willing to
devote the time and effort required to learn an alternate language in order to facilitate communication with the deaf.

The case of Nicaraguan sign language (NSL) is somewhat
different. It can't be called strictly spontaneous because it arose
in a school setting and there appear to have been outside in-
fluences, but it illustrates some of the developmental principles
at work. In this case, the emergence of a sign language has
been observed in newly created Nicaraguan schools for the
deaf. Among several cohorts of deaf children, a sign language
was seen to emerge in a situation where oral-only restrictions
at first confined signing to the children themselves and in
informal settings, beginning in the 1980s.

Senghas and her colleagues (2004) examined three cohorts of Nicaraguan signers—essentially, first-, second-, and third-generation signers—and compared their signing to the gesturing accompanying the Spanish language speech of hearing Nicaraguans. The experiment tested the idea that the signing of the older deaf signers should represent something like the language in its earliest stages, that of the second generation a more developed linguistic system, and so on. Senghas and her colleagues elicited narratives from their subjects that involved verbal expressions of path and manner of motion of objects, which, typically, are separately and sequentially encoded in spoken languages, as in "a ball rolls down a hill," but can be expressed simultaneously or sequentially in gesture or sign. Comparing the four groups of subjects—Spanish-speaking hearing gesturers and first-, second-, and third-generation signers, Senghas found that the hearing speakers never segmented their gestures for manner and path, for example, when describing something rolling down a hill; the first-generation signers infrequently segmented these gestures; and the second- and third-generation signers frequently did.

The signs and gestures illustrated in the major scientific article describing this experiment appear quite iconic, and the authors make the following observation about their findings:

> In appearance, the signs very much resemble the gestures that accompany speech. The movements of the hands and body in the sign language are clearly derived from a gestural source. Nonetheless, the analyses reveal a qualitative difference between gesturing and signing. In gesture, manner and path were integrated by expressing them simultaneously and holistically, the way they occur in the motion itself. Despite this analog, holistic nature of the gesturing that surrounded them, the first cohort of children, who started building NSL in the late 1970s, evidently introduced the possibility of dissecting out manner and path and assembling them into a sequence

of elemental units. As second and third cohorts learned the language in the mid-1980s and 1990s, they rapidly made this segmented, sequenced construction the preferred means of expressing motion events. NSL, thus, quickly acquired the discrete, combinatorial nature that is a hallmark of language. (Senghas, Kita, and Ozyurek 2004, 1780–81)

Much has been written about the importance of the emergence of this sign language as supporting the notion that the motivation to develop particular kinds of linguistic structures is genetically determined or "instinctual," especially by Steven Pinker in his best-selling book *The Language Instinct* (1994, 36–37). Further discussion of this issue follows in the next chapter.

Two cases where sign languages or systems have developed or appear to be developing where solitary deaf people have to interact with the hearing people around them end this section. The first case, reported in the early 1970s by Rolf Kuschel (1973), involved a single deaf person named Kangobai on Rennell Island in the Solomon Islands group in the South Pacific. Kangobai's case shows that even with only one signer present in a traditional society, a signing system may emerge that a substantial number of hearing people understand. Kuschel describes the signs in use as being generally iconic, and he classifies them into three categories, varying by their degrees of transparency:

1. Gestures immediately decipherable by members of other cultures.
2. Gestures immediately decipherable by members of Kangobai's own culture.
3. Gestures of a sui-generic character and immediately decipherable only by a few selected members of Kangobai's own culture.

By "sui-generic," Kuschel refers to signs that have less obvious iconicity and are understood according to convention by people who interact on a regular basis.

Finally, in an analysis of the signing of three deaf Brazilians who were not members of an extensive deaf community, Ivani Fusellier-Souza questions the commonly held view that some critical mass of deaf signers, especially in an educational facility for deaf people or a small-scale traditional society, is necessary for language-like signing to emerge. It is important to note that her conclusion is, to some extent, supported by the situation described above by Kuschel.

Fusellier-Souza calls the signing done by these deaf people "Primary Sign Languages," not to be confused with similar terminology used for another purpose by Kendon and discussed in the next section of this chapter. These appear to have been elaborated out of what have elsewhere been described as "Homesigns." Drawing on terminology introduced by Cuxac (2000), Fusellier-Souza (2006) examines the signing of these deaf people sorted into two main tracks: "illustrative (or highly iconic) signing," and "stabilized gestural signs." This suggests a distinction between ad hoc illustration of events and a set of signs that have been conventionalized (through ritualization) between the deaf signers and the (primarily) hearing people with whom they interact. According to Fusellier-Souza:

> It appears from this analysis that an initial process of iconization of experience, evidenced in these languages, follows a structured course. . The existence of gestural signs representing HIS [Highly Iconic Structures] and stabilized forms demonstrates that the bifurcation of the signers' intents into two structural branches ("telling while showing" and "telling without showing") is already at work. I have observed that the illustrative branch permits these signers not only to construct a concept in an illustrative intent when they do not

have a stabilized sign but also to elucidate, in a metalinguistic fashion, a stabilized gestural sign that has been topicalized in discourse. (2006, 46–48)

Once again, the process of linguistic emergence appears to involve the introduction of new signs through iconic resemblance to referents, followed by conventionalization through use.

Indigenous Signs

This section explores the evidence for the development and use of well-organized sign systems, if not sign languages, in nonindustrial societies even when deaf people are not generally present. Especially when these have been small-scale societies, it is safe to say that these cases have been characterized by linguistic diversity in the larger environment. In situations where the community of speakers of a particular spoken language is quite small and the community is surrounded by speakers of many other languages, a premium may be placed on developing signed systems as *linguae francae*.

European travelers during their great age of exploration found indigenous peoples in various parts of the world who could communicate using signs—in fact this was the most common way in which communication was generally established when no mutually comprehensible spoken language existed (e.g., Bonvillian, Ingram, and McCleary 2009). For example, Bonvillian et al. found numerous references to sign communication in the account by Cabeza da Vaca, a would-be Spanish conquistador, of his epic journey across what is now Texas and Mexico in 1534–1536.

The Plains Indian Sign Language is perhaps the example best known to a general audience, at least partly because of its promotion by Ernest Thompson Seton and the Boy Scouts of

America. In the course of Coronado's expedition of conquest in the 1540s, Spanish conquistadors were the first Europeans to interact with Plains Indians. According to accounts of the expedition, these Indians were so conversant in signs that they could make themselves understood without the need for interpreters (Horwitz 2008, 180). In 1803, Lewis and Clark took George Drouillard, a part Shawnee sign language interpreter, with them on their cross-continent expedition. Drouillard, communicating through sign language, helped Lewis convince the Shoshone to assist the Corps of Discovery in their passage through the Rocky Mountains:

> Commenting on Drouillard's sign language skills, Lewis, on August 14, 1805, wrote: "The means I had of communicating with these people was by way of Drewyer [Drouillard] who understood perfectly the common language of jesticulation [sic] or signs which seems to be universally understood by all the Nations we have yet seen. It is true that this language is imperfect and liable to error but is much less so than would be expected. The strong parts of the ideas are seldom mistaken." (http://www.pbs.org/lewisandclark/inside/gdrou.html)

It is not entirely clear how much of the established Plains Indian Sign Language Drouillard knew and how much his general skills in gestural communication allowed him to function successfully in these intercultural encounters. Sacagawea [aka Sacajawea], the young Shoshone woman who famously accompanied the expedition, was evidently also a skilled sign language interpreter. The caption from the reproduction of a painting reconstructing her meeting with her long lost relatives illustrates how folklore about sign language has entered the popular imagination:

> Historic moment on August 17, 1805, when, by Shoshone sign language, the Indian interpreter for Lewis and Clark is saying "I am Sacajawea," and the women of her tribe are responding,

"Sacajawea, the boat woman." (Hebard 1999, first published
1933, frontispiece)

That there was a well-established sign communication system
in use as a *lingua franca* on the Great Plains of North America
is clear from a number of other reports and studies, including
that of Garrick Mallery, published in 1881 by the Smithsonian
Institution's Bureau of Ethnology, that explicitly compared
the Plains Indian sign language to that of deaf people in use
at Gallaudet. The Plains sign language has also survived into
modern times. Brenda Farnell has documented its use among
Assiniboine women for storytelling that involves mixed use
of signing and speaking:

> It is probably the case that storytellers in all cultures use man-
> ual gestures to add meaning and dynamics to their tales, but
> the extent to which this is the case and the extent to which
> the semantic load is borne by such actions await investigation.
> . . . Among the Assiniboine or Nakota people of northern
> Montana, whose storytelling traditions provide the focus for
> this study, there are storytellers whose hand gestures draw
> upon a unique action sign system that can also be used inde-
> pendently of speech. This system has been known generally
> as Indian Sign Language but is more accurately called Plains
> Sign Talk (PST). (1995, 1)

The following example of how to make the sign for a proper
noun in Lakota comes from Mallery's 1881 study.

MISSOURI RIVER.

Make the sign for *water* by placing the right hand upright six
or eight inches in front of the mouth, back outward, index
and thumb crooked, and their ends about an inch apart, the
other fingers nearly closed; then move it toward the mouth,
and then downward nearly to the top of the breast-bone, at
the same time turning the hand over toward the mouth until
the little finger is uppermost; and the sign for *large* as follows:
The opened right hands, palms facing, fingers relaxed and

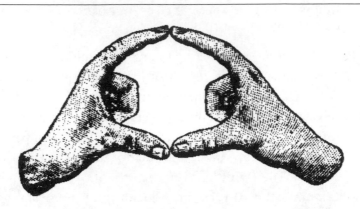

Another sign for *sun*, made by the Cheyennes, is by placing the tips of the partly separated thumb and index of one hand against those of the other, approximating a circle, and holding them toward the sky, Fig. 116, and that for *various things*, observed among the Brulé Sioux with the same position of the hands, is made by placing the circle horizontal, and moving it interruptedly toward the right side, each movement forming a short arch. Compare also the sign for *village*, described on page 386.

Fig. 11. Plains Indian sign. From Mallery 1881.

slightly separated, being at the height of the breast and about two feet apart, separate them nearly to arm's length; and then rapidly rotate the right hand from right to left several times, its back upward, fingers spread and pointing forward to show that it is stirred up or muddy. (*Dakota* IV)

As a final note, a modern study of Plains Indian Sign language was written in 1960 by La Mont West.

Another significant signing tradition is that found among aboriginal Australian women (Umiker-Sebeok and Sebeok 1978); most comprehensively documented by Adam Kendon (1988). Kendon provides detailed descriptions of sign languages

used in the North Central Desert of Australia during the
1970s and '80s, primarily by women during periods of obliga-
tory silence concurrent with male initiation and death-and-
mourning rituals. Figure 12 contains illustrations of some of
the signs used by Warlpiri women. Note the obvious iconicity
of the signs for coat and truck or car, while the source of the
sign for "shame" is not obvious. We will return repeatedly to
the theme that in sign languages (visual languages in general),
signs will tend to be iconic when they can be, but that their
inventors have no difficulty creating signs for concepts that
cannot easily be represented iconically.

Kendon categorizes the sign languages of Australia and the
Plains Indians as "alternate sign languages," to distinguish them
in scope and complexity of structure, as well as context for
use, from the "primary sign languages" of the deaf. His distinction is fairly straightforward:

> I propose that sign languages proper, as Stokoe would have it,
> be termed *primary sign languages,* while sign languages devel-
> oped by people already competent in some spoken language
> be termed *alternate sign languages.* The word 'alternate' is sug-
> gested, for these systems are typically developed for use as an
> alternative to speech in circumstances where, for whatever
> reason, speech is not used. (1988, 4)

He goes on to assert that the alternate systems used by the
people of central Australia are likely the most complex of
these alternate systems that have ever been devised.

Of particular interest for those concerned with visual expressions of symbolic activity, which seems particularly well
developed among these Australian societies, Warlpiri women
have also been observed using a complex system of sand drawing to help narrate their stories. Munn describes this activity:

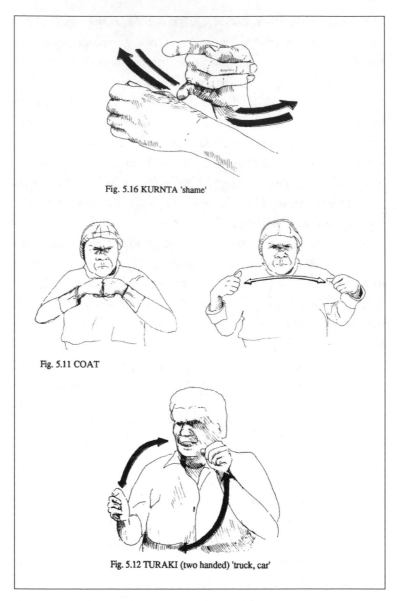

Fig. 5.16 KURNTA 'shame'

Fig. 5.11 COAT

Fig. 5.12 TURAKI (two handed) 'truck, car'

Fig. 12. Australian Aboriginal signs. From Kendon 1988, pp. 107, 110.

Both men and women draw similar graphic elements on the ground during storytelling or general discourse, but women formalize this narrative usage in a distinctive genre that I call a *sand story*. A space of about one to two feet in diameter is smoothed in the sand; the stubble is removed and small stones plucked out. The process of narration consists of the rhythmic interplay of a continuous running graphic notation with gesture signs and a singsong verbal patter. The vocal accompaniment may sometimes drop to a minimum; the basic meaning is then carried by the combination of gestural and graphic signs. The gesture signs are intricate and specific and can substitute on occasion for a fuller verbalization. (1973, 59–61)

The iconography expressed in these sand paintings, for example some of the figures shown in figure 13, now appears in the contemporary painting being done by native Australian artists.

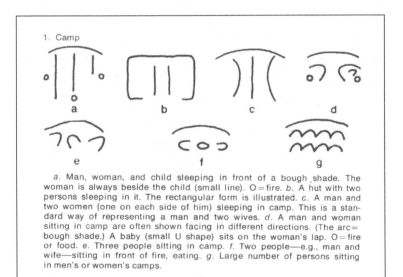

1. Camp

a. Man, woman, and child sleeping in front of a bough shade. The woman is always beside the child (small line). O = fire. b. A hut with two persons sleeping in it. The rectangular form is illustrated. c. A man and two women (one on each side of him) sleeping in camp. This is a standard way of representing a man and two wives. d. A man and woman sitting in camp are often shown facing in different directions. (The arc = bough shade.) A baby (small U shape) sits on the woman's lap. O = fire or food. e. Three people sitting in camp. f. Two people—e.g., man and wife—sitting in front of fire, eating. g. Large number of persons sitting in men's or women's camps.

Fig. 13. Australian sand story. Adapted from Munn 1973.

The Emergence of Sign Languages: Summing Up

What have we learned from the study of sign languages that have developed spontaneously either because their users were unable to hear and could not employ the usual vocal/auditory channel or because they felt another strong motivation for inventing a visual language? First and foremost, the source of most, if not all, signs is ultimately iconic or indexic—these signs arise by imitation of some object or action or by pointing to or otherwise indicating the objects to which they refer. At the most basic level, they will be as iconic, indexic, and transparent as they can be given limitations of context and extent of situations in which they are used. Second, over time, signs will become increasingly conventionalized through ritualized use and may lose much of their original iconicity, unless the iconicity is especially easily and economically expressed. This can be seen, for example, in the widespread tendency for signs referring to eating and drinking to be made near the mouth and for small numbers to be represented directly by holding up the appropriate number of fingers. It would be counterintuitive for the number 4, in any sign language, not to involve four fingers in some manner, or four beats. The medium of speech affords almost no situations where a symbol can be this obviously and directly iconic. In the case of more highly evolved sign languages or systems, where the original iconicity has been reduced or lost, the users will generally retain what might be called a "folk etymology" explaining the sources of the original iconicity. As signs become less iconic, they may retain a link to their original imagery through metaphorical processes. Nothing expressed here should be taken as implying, however, that users of sign languages have any difficulty inventing completely arbitrary signs when there is no obvious iconic relationship that can be drawn upon. Third, as the social circumstances in which these languages are used expand, they will become increasingly complex with respect to both lexicon and syntax or grammar. Fourth, in the grammatical systems of sign languages, directions of motion will be represented iconically where possible—e.g., upward motion in the event being represented will generally involve upward motion of the hands or other body parts.

4 Signing and the Language Faculty

A Modern Linguistics of Sign Language

Douglas Baynton (2002) has pointed out that prior to the oralist victory over sign-based deaf education in the late nineteenth century, there was widespread acceptance, within the intellectual community, of sign languages as comprising a legitimate form of human language, accompanied by study of their properties. For example, the French scholar Roch-Amboise Bébian published serious linguistic studies of the French sign language in the mid-nineteenth century. Baynton describes the chilling effect that the oralist movement, supported by a social Darwinian view of sign languages as primitive, had on any further serious study of them. Such was the disdain that linguists had for sign languages that Edward Sapir could say this about them in his seminal 1921 book, *Language: An Introduction to the Study of Speech:*

> Still another interesting group of transfers are the different gesture languages, developed for the use of deaf-mutes, of Trappist monks vowed to perpetual silence, or of communicating parties that are within seeing distance of each other but are out of earshot. Some of these systems are one-to-one equivalences of the normal system of speech; others, like military gesture-symbolism or the gesture language of the Plains Indians of North America (understood by tribes of mutually unintelligible forms of speech) are imperfect transfers, limiting themselves to the rendering of such grosser speech elements

as are an imperative minimum under difficult circumstances.
(p. 21)

Modern scientific study of the signed languages of the deaf
began with the work of William C. Stokoe at Gallaudet
University (then College). Stokoe was a scholar of Middle
English with a Ph.D. from Cornell University who was hired
to teach at Gallaudet in the mid-1950s. When he arrived at
Gallaudet he had no experience with deaf people or any
form of signed language. He quickly became convinced that
the conventional wisdom concerning "the sign language"
among hearing people—that it was either elaborate pantomime or a crude surrogate for English—was inaccurate and
insufficient.

From the outset of his work to describe and analyze what
came to be known as American Sign Language, Stokoe realized that it would shed light on the nature of language in
general. Stokoe is often described as having "discovered" ASL
or as having "proved" that ASL is a language. A good deal of
mythology has sprung up around this question, and, to some
extent, Stokoe felt about it the way Columbus should have felt
when he was described as having "discovered" America. Just
as American Indians had known about the Americas for more
than 10,000 years before Columbus arrived, so deaf people
had been aware of the "languageness" of their signing and of
the benefits that it conferred long before Stokoe came on the
scene. They were also "proving" that it was a real language on
a daily basis by using it to perform all of the functions that
languages usually perform. But just as Columbus had done
with respect to the scope of the physical world, Stokoe's ac-
complishment was to reveal these facts to a larger, skeptical
public; and, in doing so, he made a "Columbian" addition to

our knowledge of the linguistic world and to our understanding of the human condition.

One aspect of Stokoe's genius was to recognize that it would not be good enough simply to announce the "good news" that sign language was really a language—he would need to show it using the tools of the science of language, the tools of descriptive linguistics. As we have seen, Noam Chomsky launched a revolution in linguistic science in the mid-1950s. As a result of this intellectual revolution, language, or the human capacity to produce and decode it, came to be seen more as the expression of a hard-wired language organ or "faculty" than as a social phenomenon. However, Stokoe was mainly influenced by an older anthropological linguistics that had as its most urgent goal describing exotic languages that were facing extinction. Anthropological linguists, and anthropologists in general for that matter, had for a half century been trying to overcome Western prejudices that depicted non-Western languages as inferior to those of Europe. These scholars had developed an armamentarium that could be used to describe any spoken language and transcribe it to paper.

They had come to realize that all languages have regular structures at a level below that of the individual word—according to the terminology of linguistics, they have sublexical or phonological structure. This structure is based upon systems of contrast—differences in meaning must be based upon perceptible differences in language sounds, as in *bat* and *hat*. It is this sublexical structure that makes phonetic writing possible, and all spoken languages have it. Stokoe's masterstroke was to show that ASL has such a structure and that it too can be written in a phonetic-like script (Stokoe 1960; Stokoe, Casterline, and Croneberg 1965). By devising a workable script, he was able to convince other language scholars that ASL employs such a system of linguistic contrast, that it has a regular internal structure, and that it is, therefore, not simply ad-hoc pantomime or a corrupt visual code for English (see fig. 14). It is beyond the scope of this discussion to describe Stokoe's system in detail (see, for example, Armstrong 1999), but it is worth noting that it has held up well, despite numerous attempts to improve upon it, and is still used to transcribe signed languages. Stokoe, along with two deaf colleagues, Carl Croneberg and Dorothy Casterline, used this notation system to compile the first comprehensive dictionary of ASL in 1965.

Having completed this initial descriptive work, Stokoe then set about to convince the larger world, especially educators and linguists, of the linguistic qualities of ASL—he took these ideas "on the road" so to speak. At Gallaudet he put in place several operations that would further bolster the legitimacy of ASL and other sign languages. First, he set up the Linguistics Research Laboratory in 1971 and invited people from around the world to work on problems in the description and interpretation of sign languages. This provided an institutional home for sign language research. Second, in 1972, he founded the journal *Sign Language Studies* to provide an outlet for publication of increasingly complex and sophisticated scholarly articles on linguistic and other aspects of the signed languages of the deaf. At the time, mainstream linguistic journals showed little interest in publishing work from this incipient field.

During the early 1970s, Stokoe began to see that his work on ASL might have a larger significance, beyond the development of increasingly complex linguistic studies and the support these were providing for the reform of deaf education. At

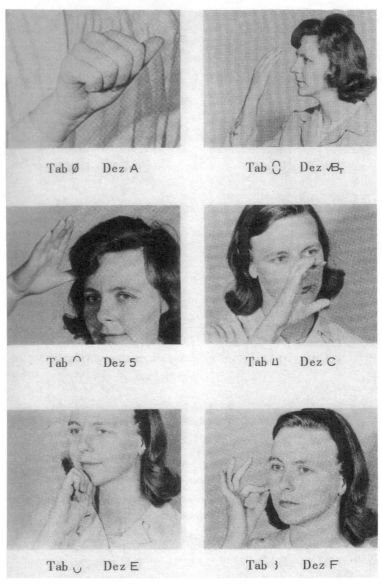

Fig. 14. Examples of Stokoe's notational system—Tab stands for "tabula" and refers to the location in which the sign is made and Dez stands for "designator" and refers to the configuration of the hand making it. From Stokoe, Casterline, and Croneberg 1965.

this time, Stokoe became interested in the newly reinvigorated scientific study of the origin and evolution of the human capacity for language. Because this topic had been the subject of rampant and undisciplined speculation around the turn of the twentieth century, it had fallen out of favor with linguists and anthropologists. Stokoe joined a small group of scholars, including Gordon Hewes, Charles Hockett, Roger Wescott, Stevan Harnad, Jane Lancaster, and Horst Steklis, who began to synthesize new information from paleontology, primatology, neuroscience, linguistics, and, significantly, sign language studies into more coherent scenarios for the evolution of language (see Harnad, Steklis, and Lancaster 1976). During the past forty years, these scenarios have grown more sophisticated and plausible, due in large part to Stokoe's efforts.

Stokoe concerned himself especially with evolutionary problems that might be solved by postulating a signing stage in human evolution. He participated in several important symposia on this topic, one of which resulted in the book *Language Origins* (Wescott 1974). In order to get this book into print, Stokoe established a small publishing company, Linstok Press, which also took over publication of the journal *Sign Language Studies.* Stokoe came to believe that iconic manual gesture must have played a key role in the transition from prehuman primate communication to human language, whether signed or spoken. In making this assertion, he was rediscovering a line of thinking, as we have already seen, that can be traced back at least to the Abbé de Condillac, an influential figure in the French enlightenment of the eighteenth century.

According to this line of thinking, the introduction of iconic manual gesture might solve the problem of attribution of meaning to arbitrary vocal signals—iconic gestures which resemble the things they refer to might form a bridge to the symbolic relationship of speech sounds to their referents. This might occur if iconic gestures became paired with noniconic sounds in reference to objects and events in the environment. But Stokoe went a step beyond this to suggest that iconic manual gestures might also have been involved in the thornier question of the origin of syntax. This goes to the question at the heart of Chomskyan linguistics, which posits syntax as the defining characteristic of human languages—how do languages come to refer not only to objects and events, but to the infinite number of possible relationships among them?

What is essentially at stake here is the very nature of the human language "faculty" itself. What not only enables us to create our complex languages, but, in effect demands that we do so? Every human society creates and uses language, and, as we have seen, this includes social groups of deaf people using a visual/gestural medium that lies outside the oral/aural medium used by most hearing people as their principal channel for language. Chomsky's solution to the problem was to posit that there must be a genetically determined language organ in the brain that operates according to essentially the same abstract principles in every human brain. Individual languages, then, are the expressions of this language organ following the principles of a "universal grammar." All languages could be seen as highly constrained and having basically the same organizing principles. Stokoe (and Chomsky) understood that sign languages provided a possible test case of this universalist theory. It could be argued that a symbiotic relationship eventually emerged between Chomskyan universalist theory and a branch of sign language linguistic theory. If signed languages could be seen as having exactly the same abstract organizing principles as spoken languages, the Chomskyan theory of genetically based grammar rules would be reinforced as would the linguistic status of sign languages generally (see Pinker 1994, 152–53). As we will see later, Stokoe came to argue that the linguistic status of ASL and other signed languages was not dependent on this sort of structural identity.

The initial thrust of much of the linguistic study of ASL was directed at showing at least a functional (if not a structural) equivalence between signed and spoken language—as we saw earlier, Stokoe focused on identifying a sublexical structure of ASL similar to that of spoken languages. One of the major principles of modern linguistics is that the symbols of language are arbitrary—they are connected to what they refer to by convention only and not by some sort of resemblance (often called iconic). This posed an obvious problem for linguists trying to show structural equivalence between sign and speech—it is clear that many, if not all (in this regard, see Bouvet 1997), sign language signs are iconic or "motivated" in some way, as linguists might put it. For example, in many sign languages, signs for food involve actions of the hands around the mouth.

Certain translation practices (e.g., using "glossing," suggesting one-to-one correspondences between sign language signs and the words of a spoken language) may lead to the assumption that functional similarity or even equivalence is the same as structural or formal equivalence—to accomplish the same tasks, do sign languages necessarily have to have the exactly the same grammatical components as spoken languages? In response to this question, Dan Slobin issues the following caveat:

> Clearly, ideas can be conveyed in a visual language by uses of location and motion that are simply not available to an

auditory language. We don't have a "revolution in sign language linguistics" if we begin with knowing what we are looking for—and then find it.

My favorite way of thinking about the risk of finding what you're looking for comes from my friend Wolfgang Klein, who is a German linguist who has worked on Chinese. He points out that linguists must be careful about expecting to find similar grammatical categories in unfamiliar languages. He disagrees with the general assumption of Western linguists that Chinese must have verbs because we are used to languages that have verbs. He suggests that Chinese doesn't make a clear noun/verb distinction. . . . In a striking analogy, Klein suggests that Germans know that every cuisine includes potatoes, so it is no surprise to find that the Chinese cuisine also relies on potatoes. It's just that their potatoes come in small grains and grow differently! Rice can be made to fit into the category of potatoes—but only if you ignore everything else that you know about rice. (2008, 121–28)

Armstrong describes the problem with assuming structural equivalence on the basis of functional equivalence between ASL and English, and the role of "glossing" in possibly creating confusion:

Perhaps even more apropos is another example that would generally be considered an ASL sentence consisting of three signs, and glossed into English as VEHICLE GO-AROUND PERSON, or translated into English as, "The car goes around the person. . . ." [T]his sentence consists of one hand in the 3 handshape moving around the upright index finger of the other hand. The motion is continuous and both hands, with their given shapes, are again continuously in the field of vision of the interlocutors. But how can we segment this sentence into its constituent signs? The "verb" glossed as GO-AROUND is simply the continuous action . . . of the 3 hand. (1999, 93–94)

So, where are the "nouns" and where is the "verb" in this simple sentence? Are these really genetically determined and necessary structural elements of all languages, or are we instead seeing human creativity at work, using the raw materials at hand in these vastly different media, to solve similar communication problems.

Although Stokoe was no fan of Chomskyan linguistics, an interesting parallel can be found between his later thinking and that of Chomsky. Stokoe began to see in the complex linguistic devices that were being introduced to get around the problem of iconicity an unnecessary and ultimately unproductive obscurantism. In response to this trend, in 1991 he published an extraordinarily original article entitled "Semantic Phonology." At the same time, Chomsky was moving in the direction of a "minimalist program" for generative linguistics (Chomsky 1995). According to this program, the number of essential linguistic parameters could be reduced to two: a logical form and a phonetic form. Stokoe, on the other hand, proposed that all of the multilayered complexity that had been introduced in linguistic descriptions of sign languages could be also be reduced to two parameters: something acting (in the case of manual gesture, a hand) and its action. Stokoe pointed out, moreover, that this acting unit had the essential characteristics of one of Chomsky's elementary sentences, a noun phrase plus a verb phrase. The final link in his chain of reasoning is that the use of such iconic manual gestures by early humans might have led them to analyze the agent/action relationship inherent in these gestures, leading ultimately to the elaboration of syntax and, hence, language. Through this process of analysis, early humans might also have seen that complete iconic gestures could be reduced to component parts, analogous to the phonemes and morphemes of speech, to be recombined into new and ever more complex meaningful arrangements. His views on these and many other issues are summed up in his final major work, the book *Language in Hand,* published posthumously by Gallaudet University Press (2001).

Soon after Stokoe's early work appeared (his first major publication was *Sign Language Structure* in 1960), other scholars—linguists and psychologists in particular—began to become interested in sign languages. Two scientists at the Salk Institute in San Diego, Edward Klima and Ursula Bellugi, began to publish important work on the structure and neurological underpinnings of ASL (see Klima and Bellugi 1979). This work and work by the Canadian neurologist Doreen Kimura (1981) demonstrated that language structures in the left hemisphere of the brain generally associated with speech are recruited for use in signing by deaf signers. It has also been argued that neurological involvement in the production and comprehension of sign language is probably widely distributed throughout the brain (e.g., Armstrong and Katz 1981), but the neurolinguistic work on ASL that was initiated by Klima and Bellugi has been hugely influential. In particular, in another major work, they argued that their research provided solid evidence for highly specific genetic determination of universal rules for grammar (Poizner, Klima, and Bellugi 1987).

Stokoe's contributions to the emerging study of a linguistics of sign language have recently been documented and described by Susan Lloyd McBurney (2001). She maintains that Stokoe's role was not initially given the recognition it was due by the linguistics establishment of the day, although his work on ASL may have been known to many in the field. In this regard, it is probably significant that his early work was not published in the major outlets for linguistic research. Why is this important? In science generally, precedence is all important—recognition of original work is a primary motivating force for those who undertake pioneering work in wholly new areas or who introduce revolutionary theoretical ideas.

A central question has emerged from the linguistic and neurological study of sign language use—is language in general controlled by a single "center" in the brain that determines the fundamental rules of all languages, or are its structures influenced by or dependent in some way on the medium of transmission? Stokoe became a champion of the position that the ultimate structure taken by a particular sign language is highly dependent on the visual/gestural medium in which it is transmitted (Stokoe 1991). There is a related evolutionary question: If human language depends upon uniquely human genetic determination, is there any sense in looking to our nearest genetic relatives for insight into its origin and evolution? Steven Pinker, leading proponent of genetic determinism, suggests not. Others, including Stokoe and the current author, have argued otherwise, as will be outlined in the next section.

Signing Apes

The use of a modified form of a *human* language by nonhumans, albeit, specifically, those nonhumans most closely related to us is relevant to this book's main topic. By teaching apes to use human signs, researchers hoped to shed light on the linguistic capabilities of the common ancestor of humans and apes; thereby, perhaps, increasing our understanding of the evolutionary path taken by our hominid ancestors. It opens, in other words, a window on our common heritage as communicating species, and it also affords a unique opportunity to answer some of the questions raised about the nature of genetic control for the human capacity to create and comprehend languages.

Almost from the outset of the publication of Stokoe's early linguistic studies, it occurred to primate behavioral researchers that language training with apes that involved sign language might prove more fruitful than the largely failed experiments with speech that had previously been attempted. The psychologists Allen and Beatrix Gardner were the first to make major claims of success in this endeavor with the chimpanzee Washoe in the early 1970s (see Gardner, Gardner, and Van Cantfort 1989 for a summary of this work; and King 2008 for appreciation of the significance of Washoe's linguistic achievements). Washoe and other chimps raised in a sign language environment by the Gardners were said to be capable of acquiring and appropriately using an extensive vocabulary of signs and of combining them into simple phrases (Gardner, Gardner, and Nichols 1989). It is easy to see why language origins theorists would find this research to be of exceptional importance. If chimpanzees, bonobos, and gorillas are able to produce and comprehend significant aspects of a human language, then it would be reasonable to infer that a common ancestor also possessed these capabilities. And, if those capabilities were evident with respect to signed language and not speech, then the gestural hypothesis of language origins would be strongly reinforced. It is noted that the fact that it took human intervention for these apes to use signs is thought to undermine this argument. However, evolutionary arguments generally depend heavily on the idea of unused capacity, sometimes called "preadaptation," becoming expressed under appropriate environmental conditions. Genetic variation within a population with respect to such preadaptations could be regarded as the raw material of biological evolution.

By the same token, the more chimpanzees can accomplish of a language-like nature, the less strong is the case for unique genetic determination for human linguistic capacities.

Controversy about the meaning of this ape language research arose fairly quickly. A major challenge to the Gardners came from Herbert Terrace and the "Nim Chimpsky" project (Terrace et al. 1979). Charges and countercharges followed, as to whether apes can be said to refer symbolically, to have grammar or proto-grammar, and so on. Terrace, in particular, challenged the notion that chimpanzees might be capable of using a sort of grammar (see Terrace et al. 1979; Wallman 1992; Gardner, Gardner, and Van Cantfort 1989; Premack 1986; Pinker 1994; Fouts and Mills 1997). In addition, some deaf people knowledgeable about these studies were not necessarily convinced that the trained chimpanzees were really producing ASL (Neisser 1983, 212–16). Nor could one expect that what the apes produced would be flawless human signing—as we saw in the first chapter, they have, for example, hands that are quite unlike those of humans in several critical respects.

What one makes of this evidence tends to depend on which of two fundamentally different models of the nature of language one adheres to. These approaches have been characterized as "Chomskyan" vs. "Whorfian," after the American linguist Benjamin Lee Whorf, famous for the so-called linguistic relatively hypothesis (Armstrong 1999, 47), and the distinction might now also be characterized as generativist ("Chomskyan") vs. cognitivist ("Whorfian"). In other words, there appears to be at least a connection in spirit if not in actual tradition between earlier relativistic anthropological linguistics and the current cognitive linguistic movement. It seems fair to say that the generativist school of linguistics has tended to see a greater gulf between humans and apes, that is, primarily discontinuity in evolutionary terms, while cognitivists and the more anthropologically oriented have tended to see any commonalities as indicative of evolutionary continuity.

Why is this discussion important here? Because of the symbiotic political relationship between early sign language research and the Chomskyan linguistic approach, the postulated structural identity between signed and spoken languages was taken as supportive of the notion that human beings have genetically instantiated grammar modules in their brains (see, e.g., Pinker 1994, 349), which apes are assumed not to have. Instead of supporting the idea of a genetically determined grammar module in the brain, as was first assumed by neurolinguists such as Klima and Bellugi, the new, richer analyses of signed languages that are now emerging tend to undermine it. Ultimately, if we are interested in the biological evolution of our species, we will want to know just what humans have acquired genetically if we are to understand our evolution from a generalized ape "platform." If no such grammar module exists, then there is nothing to account for at this level of specificity and a more general increment in cognitive flexibility, accompanying expansion of the brain, may be all that is needed to account for human language. The controversy over the meaning of ape language research also highlights the difficulty in distinguishing language from nonlanguage. For example, if arbitrariness of the linguistic sign is a prerequisite, if language is required to be a completely abstract code, then a large proportion of what deaf people do when they sign to each other may not qualify. This appears, fundamentally, to be an unproductive debate, and more nuanced interpretations have begun to emerge with fine-grained observation of actual ape gestural behavior (Tanner and Byrne 1996, 1999; King 2004).

How should we interpret ape communication? How do we know if we have properly construed an ape's meaning and vice versa—a problem also faced whenever we attempt to translate one *human* language into another, let alone try to understand what a member of a different species might be up to? One thing is abundantly clear—we share with apes an extremely rich and flexible social life that is mediated by visible gestures and vocalizations, and it is possible to see commonalities in social life between apes and modern human societies that employ relatively uncomplicated technologies, so called hunter-gatherers (see Armstrong, Stokoe, and Wilcox 1995). All early human beings lived in this manner for much of their existence as a separate lineage—that is, in small groups without permanent settlements and without control of the resources supporting their subsistence. In these societies all of the members would have known each other and would have been involved in constant face-to-face interaction.

We are only now beginning to learn how apes communicate through the pioneering work of researchers such as Barbara King (2004), working with gorillas in a zoo setting. Sadly this research with apes will increasingly have to be done in zoos because of the growing threat to their viability in natural settings in Africa. With respect to the principal thesis being advanced here, it is worth repeating what King (2004, 99) has to say about the gestural behavior of apes under captive conditions, "The studies by Savage-Rumbaugh and colleagues [1977] and Tanner and Byrne [1999], then, demonstrate co-regulated gestural communication in African apes, and suggest iconicity in their gestures."

King goes on to point out, commenting on whether or not such "iconic" gestures are really iconic from the point of view of the apes themselves or only from that of human

Fig. 15. Bonobo grooming. Courtesy of Dr. Simone Pika, Max Planck Institute for Ornithology, Seewiesen, Germany.

observers, that what really matters is how the apes use these gestures to regulate their social life (see fig. 15). In the final analysis, this issue is not fundamentally different from that of the significance of the iconicity in sign languages discussed earlier—following conventionalization of the sign, the signer may not have conscious access to its original iconicity or any communicative need for such access.

This work is critical because, as noted in the first chapter, humans and apes share a fundamental adaptation to cooperative social life. Human beings have certainly become increasingly dependent on technology, but there is little doubt that for most of our history our ancestors relied fundamentally on the ability to organize for productive activity more than they relied on tools. For example, the highly successful and morphologically diverse australopithecines left virtually no evidence of technology of any sort during their two million years or more on Earth—they must have been relying on the ability to communicate so as to support complex cooperative behavior. If we are going to look for the roots of language, we would be highly advised to look at the social communication of the African apes.

Interpretations of this sort of evidence usually lead to one of two general theories about the origin of language, what we have, in an acknowledged oversimplification, referred to as the continuity/discontinuity bifurcation (see, e.g., King and Shanker 1997). Pinker, in his 1994 book *The Language Instinct* states the discontinuity position most succinctly:

> [I]f human language is unique in the modern animal kingdom, as it appears to be, the implications for a Darwinian account of its evolution would be as follows: none. A language instinct unique to modern humans poses no more of a paradox than a trunk unique to modern elephants. (342)

And, by the same token, according to this view, the behavior of apes, however complex, should tell us essentially nothing about the evolution of the human capacity for language or its neurological underpinnings.

King and Shanker present the opposing (continuity) view:

> Continuity and discontinuity should be seen as orthogonal approaches to significantly different questions. The former is really asking about the origins of linguistic behavior. This differs in an essential way from asking, as does discontinuity theory, about the origin of language. For in broadening the issue to consider linguistic behavior, the continuity theorist is asking what monkeys, apes, and hominids really do—how they structure and use their communicative behavior of all types— and not just whether they can communicate in the same way as humans. Human linguistic behavior is thus situated within the much broader context of primate social behavior.

Certainly, no nonhuman primate species has shown any inclination to create the sort of behavioral, that is linguistic and cultural, diversity that we see among modern humans, but vast cultural diversity among human populations is a relatively recent phenomenon, as far as we know. Human beings with the same genetic endowment as ours did not change very much, or diversify culturally, for tens of thousands of years, at least as far as the archaeological record is concerned; and there is evidence that apes haven't changed as much genetically as humans have since the divergence of the African ape and hominid lineages (see, Armstrong and Wilcox 2007). So, it seems quite plausible that the behavior of modern apes, whether under naturalistic or experimental conditions, might have quite a bit to tell us, after all.

We can follow King in expressing appreciation for the "linguistic" achievements of apes without abandoning critical appraisal of their significance. King (2008, 318) has this to say about Washoe's achievements in the use of signs (in a statement of appreciation following Washoe's death in 2007):

> I do not take the view that Washoe "acquired a human language," as the Friends of Washoe page at the website for Central Washington University (CWU)'s Chimp and Human Communication Institute claims.[1] This statement seems to me of a wholly different nature than a claim that Washoe "uses language," or "uses elements of language," which is well-supported by the evidence. Of course, a nonhuman animal may someday fully master a human language, but to date, none has. No ape creates poetry or tells stories about the past using ASL or any other language, for example. To say that Washoe "acquired ASL" is, I believe, wrong, and just as importantly, leads us to miss the genuine significance of what she has done with language.

King (2008) goes on to summarize what Washoe was able to achieve with signs and this summary applies equally to

---

1. http://www.friendsofwashoe.org/washoe_bio.shtml

Fig. 16. Washoe with Beatrix Gardner. From Gardner, Gardner, and Van Cantfort 1989, p. 56. Reprinted by permission of SUNY Press. Copyright 1989.

some other "signing" apes. These achievements include the following:

1. Washoe was able to use about 170 signs;
2. She was able to create names for things for which she did not know a sign;
3. She was able to express empathy through signs;
4. She had a tendency to sign to herself;
5. She was able to teach signs to her adoptive son, Loulis;
6. Washoe and her ape companions used signs among themselves.

The Biological Basis and Structure of Sign Languages: Summing Up

Sign languages arise readily among human populations and can be learned to a limited extent even by apes, given appropriate circumstances. Neurological studies show that the neural apparatus generally used to support speech can readily be adapted for use in the production and comprehension of signed languages. Moreover, given the enormous plasticity of the human brain, other parts of the brain can be recruited for this purpose as well. The governing principle being advanced here is a utilitarian and functional one—human societies have an overwhelming drive to construct languages that are adequate to the social purposes for which they are created. It is clear, moreover, that to accomplish this end we will use whatever raw materials, visible or audible, available within our communities. It is also clear that symbols of all languages, signed or spoken, will be iconic when they can be, as in sign, and arbitrary when they must be, as in speech.

5 Deaf Gain: Visible Language in the Modern World

THIS CHAPTER CONSIDERS the modern growth of understanding about the visual bases of language generally. We will also trace the evolution of the dissemination of language in the visual mode, which has grown with the technological innovations of the twentieth and twenty-first centuries, as well as the contribution that the deaf experience makes to our understanding of how to use visual modes of communication in general. We start in what seems at first to be an unlikely place—consideration of an influential work of literary theory from the early twentieth century.

A recently released volume includes an original essay by Ernest Fenollosa, "The Chinese Written Character as a Medium for Poetry," on the relevance of Chinese writing to modern poetry, along with the well-known 1919 posthumous version edited by Ezra Pound, and a critical essay by Haun Saussy (2008). The volume also contains additional pieces by Fenollosa. Many scholars consider the central piece in the volume, Pound's edited version of Fenollosa's original essay, to be an important source document for Imagism, a central force in the development of Modernist poetry early in the twentieth century. However, the essay has been roundly criticized by scholars of the Chinese language for naively representing the Chinese writing system as "ideographic" or pictorial. Saussy argues that the essay is better understood not as a serious analysis of the system of Chinese characters (although Pound's alterations may make it seem less serious in this regard than Fenollosa originally intended), but as a philosophical manifesto on the nature of human language in general and poetry in particular. Of special interest is its exposition of the nature of the visual perception of reality that inevitably underlies language of all kinds, whether it is ultimately expressed audibly or visually. In this regard, Fenollosa/Pound take up many of the concepts that later become important in the cognitive movement in linguistics—especially iconicity, gesture, and metaphor.

Pound's goal was to strip away the frills and trappings of the Victorian era in poetry from which the Western world was emerging at the beginning of the twentieth century. Pound was thus led to announce an "ideogrammic" method, to show how abstraction could arise from concrete visual images. According to Saussy, in this regard Pound, through his understanding of Fenollosa, saw Chinese writing as a model for "valid thinking."

> [Fenollosa] got to the root of the matter, to the root of the difference between what is valid in Chinese thinking and invalid or misleading in a great deal of European thinking and language.
>
> The simplest statement I can make of his meaning is as follows:
>
> In Europe, if you ask a man to define anything, his definition always moves away from the simple things that he knows perfectly well, it recedes into an unknown region, that is a region of remoter and progressively remoter abstraction.
>
> Thus if you ask him what red is, he says it is a 'color.'
>
> If you ask him what a color is, he tells you it is vibration or a refraction of light, or a division of the spectrum.
>
> If you ask him what vibration is, he tells you it is a mode of energy, or something of that sort, until you arrive at a modality of being, or non-being, at any rate you get in beyond your depth, and beyond his depth. . . .

The Chinese will use abbreviated pictures AS pictures, that is to say, Chinese ideogram does not try to be the picture of a sound, or to be a written sign recalling a sound, but it is still the picture of a thing; of a thing in a given position or relation, or of a combination of things. It means the thing or the action or situation, or quality germane to the several things that it pictures. . . .

He is to define red. How can he do it in a picture that isn't painted in red paint?

He puts (or his ancestor put) together the abbreviated pictures of

ROSE   CHERRY
IRON RUST   FLAMINGO

That, you see, is very much the kind of thing a biologist does . . . when he gets together a few hundred or thousand slides, and picks out what is necessary for his general statement. (Saussy, Stalling, and Klein 2008, 4–5)

Thus, according to Fenollosa/Pound, the Chinese character for red is only a partial abstraction derived from concrete images of red objects of various shades. Again, this represents a distortion of the actual Chinese writing system, which *does* represent actual Chinese spoken words and *does* incorporate phonetic cues in its system of characters. But, again, following Saussy's analysis, this is not what is potentially interesting and important about the essay. Saussy sees this significance in the essay's, in effect, cross-cultural critique of the Western poetry of the time and Pound's use of this critique in the creation of a new poetic vision.

The significance of the essay for readers of this book may lie instead in its presentation of a "visucentric" view of the underpinnings of human language in general and the relationship of this visucentrism to an evolving modern poetics. Within this view, we can see that there are similarities between signing and the Chinese writing system. In both cases, "folk etymologies" exist for the origins of what are now nontransparent and conventionalized visual symbols, as illustrated by the example of "red" above. Similarly, there is a belief in something like the concrete—abstract axis of sign/ character evolution or an iconic—arbitrary axis through processes of conventionalization. Along with a persistent belief in these historical processes by their users, both systems likewise involve structured, componential use of "phonological" underpinnings. In addition, researchers occasionally claim that Chinese characters have influenced or been influenced by sign language signs (Nakamura 2006, 17).

As developed in Fenollosa/Pound, much of the expression of this argument concerning the visual foundations of language appears somewhat archaic, but it has historical interest as illustrative of an ongoing branch of thought about the origin and nature of language that connects to early theories of the possible origins of language in visual gesture and to modern thinking about the cognitive underpinnings of language in general. For treatment of the direct relevance of Fenollosa's analysis to the study of sign languages, see Dirksen Bauman's doctoral dissertation (1998).

However, it is strikingly evident that the visual has recently gained a quantum advantage in human communication that could not have been predicted by Alexander Graham Bell, the Steve Jobs of his day, let alone Fenollosa and Pound. The computer and Internet revolution has wrought changes that can only be reversed by a complete collapse of our modern technological culture. But this revolution was preceded by a longer and perhaps even more significant penetration of the general culture by visual images of all kinds, especially photographic and cinematic, and by a rise in the importance of gesture in these visible presentations. In this regard, and as a prelude to

Fig. 17. A static, medium shot of a tree centrally located in the frame from the ASL poem, "A Lone, Sturdy, Tree," by Clayton Valli. Reprinted from Bauman 2003, p. 40. Illustration by Dr. Jennifer Nelson, Gallaudet University.

the discussion of the concept of "deaf gain" that appears in the next section, it is worth noting that scholars of sign language have begun to point to the explicitly "cinematic" nature of signed presentations. In a discussion of the cinematic structure of ASL poetry (see fig. 17), Bauman credits Stokoe with first making this comparison. According to Stokoe:

> In a signed language . . . narrative is no longer linear and prosaic. Instead, the essence of sign language is to cut from a normal view to a close-up to a distant shot to a close-up again, and so on, even including flashback and flash-forward scenes, exactly as a movie editor works. (Bauman 2003, 36)

It may be no accident that deaf actors were among the early cast members of silent films (Schuchman 2004, 233–34). Silent films, of course, which were captioned, gave deaf people a brief period of equality of access to a new communication technology that was eliminated with the introduction of talking films. Even given the introduction of "talkies," deaf people found ways to use the new motion picture technology for their own purposes—these included production of films designed to preserve examples of the use of ASL by master signers, in films dating to the turn of the twentieth century, and films produced for the entertainment of the deaf community itself (Schuchman 2004).

Next we will consider the work of the sociologist Erving Goffman, who was best known for his work on the nature of the intricate face-to-face interactions that support human social behavior. Here, we will focus on his work on the presentation of visual images in the mass media in his book *Gender Advertisements* (1987) to convey a particular symbolism concerning the nature of gender differences. Goffman presents the scope of this work in these terms:

> Assume all of an individual's behavior and appearance informs those who witness him, minimally telling them something about his social identity, about his mood, intent, and expectations, and about the state of his relation to them. In every culture a distinctive range of this indicative behavior and appearance becomes specialized so as to more routinely and perhaps more effectively perform this informing function, the informing coming to be the controlling role of the performance, although often not avowedly so. One can call these indicative events [borrowing a term from the study of animal behavior] displays. . . . If gender be defined as the culturally established correlates of sex (whether in consequence of biology or learning), then gender display refers to conventionalized portrayals of these correlates. (1)

Goffman argues persuasively, with most of his visual evidence coming from magazine advertisements published during the 1960s and early '70s, that a pervasive visual symbolism of gender is readily decoded by the audience allowing for mass dissemination of advertising material—this symbolism being conveyed largely by facial expression, body positioning, and, of special interest here, positioning and shape of the hands (see fig. 18). The Internet has led to an enormous increase

Fig. 18. These photographs illustrate a gesture discussed by Goffman (1987: 60): "Just as covering the mouth with the hand can be an attenuation of covering the face, so a finger brought to the mouth can be an attenuation of covering it with the hand. But here another ritualization seems more common: the attenuation of sucking or biting the finger. The impression is given that somehow a stream of anxiety, rumination, or whatever, has been split off from the main course of attention and is being sustained in a dissociated, unthinking fashion. In any case the face is partly covered as though one could see but not be seen and were therefore free to engage hand and face outside the stream of face-to-face address." Images from www.featurepics.com.

in the capacity to disseminate visual information, including video, and in the capacity for this sort of symbolism to be used to influence the behavior of mass audiences.

Deaf Gain

With a revolution underway in the ability of human beings to communicate at a distance in real time through the visual medium, discussion of a concept called "deaf gain" has begun at Gallaudet University. Deaf gain can be thought of as the conceptual opposite of "hearing loss" (Bauman and Murray 2009). In other words, we can ask what the deaf experience of many centuries has contributed to the sum total of useful knowledge about the human condition in general, and especially about the human capacity to communicate using the visual medium.

This concept can fit into a larger scientific framework, an evolutionary one. At the outset of any evolutionary discussion of deafness, we might ask whether or not its genetic causes have been selected against, as we would expect if it is a truly deleterious condition. The answer appears to be no—as we have seen there are many historically documented instances of substantial deaf populations with continuity through many generations. In fact, eugenicists at the turn of the twentieth century, including Alexander Graham Bell, feared the opposite—that genetically caused deafness might actually be increasing in the general population.

The fundamental problem in the study of evolution is to show how a species has overcome the second law of thermodynamics—that entropy or disorganization is always increasing in a physical system. The American reformer Sylvester Graham stated this principle, with respect to living systems, most succinctly and aptly in 1854 (43): "From the commencement to the termination of the vital existence of organized bodies, therefore, life maintains a continual conflict with opposing forces: and hence it has with beauty and propriety been said, 'that life is a forced state'—'a temporary victory over the causes which induce death.'" (The economist John Maynard Keynes has stated this principle even more concisely: "In the long run we are all dead.") Five years later, in 1859, Darwin described the biological process, natural selection of genetically more fit individuals, by which this organization is introduced and sustained.

As the members of a species reproduce through successive generations, they are constantly overcoming entropy. The answer to how they are able to do this is an evolutionary process, whereby energy input can lead to the extraction, coding, storage, and eventual decoding of information within the system. While the process can have a fundamentally random basis, as in genetic mutation, there must also be a process for identifying and storing random bits of potentially useful information. In a biological system, this occurs through the process of natural selection—a very slow process, as it depends on the random production of advantageous mutations, and the propagation and storage of these mutations across many generations, within specific environmental niches.

Human cultures can greatly expedite and speed up the process of information storage, especially when they are able to use language. Evolution can then occur at the level of culture, and, because it now depends on stored knowledge and not random genetic change, it can be purposeful and goal directed, necessity being the mother of invention. Within this framework, we see language as primarily a mechanism for encoding useful information, and prior to the invention of writing, for storing it within the collective heads of a community for intergenerational transmission to future generations. Part of the beauty of this system is that language allows for a division of labor with respect to the storage of parts of the collective pool of information. Different members of the community can remember different pieces of what is useful to know about the social structure and physical environment of the community. This is a partial explanation (sometimes called the grandmother hypothesis) for the tendency of human societies to preserve their elders, especially women, well beyond the end of their reproductive years, a challenge for a purely biological evolutionary theory that entails the propagation of genetic changes that result in the enhancement of reproductive success. According to this view, a community's elders will have observed and remembered a great deal having to do with the ecological and social conditions vital to their community's survival. For example, a nomadic society might depend upon locating fruiting trees at exactly the moment when the fruit is ripe. This sort of information could be held by the elders—but it would only become accessible to the rest of the community through language. The society's survival, then, would be enhanced by possessing and having easy access to information that was acquired by a process of trial and error over many generations.

Writing about the accelerating process by which many of the world's languages are becoming extinct, K. David Harrison comments on the analogy between biological and linguistic evolution:

> Extending the biological metaphor, language disappearance only superficially resembles species extinction. Animal species are complex, have evolved over long periods of time, possess unique traits, and have adapted to a specific ecological niche. An extinct dodo bird can be stuffed by taxidermists and dis-

played in a museum after all its kind are dead and gone. But a
stuffed dodo is no substitute for a thriving dodo population.
Languages, too, have adapted over time to serve the needs of
a particular population in their environment. They have been
shaped by people to serve as repositories for cultural knowledge, efficiently packaged and readily transmittable across generations. (2007, 81–86)

While many of world's sign languages are similarly endan-
gered, that issue will not be addressed here. The compelling
case for their continuing value and for preserving them has
been made elsewhere (Johnston 2004).

Deaf gain represents the experience of signing deaf communities collected and stored over many generations and
coded for future extraction in sign languages. The reading
out of this experience tells us much about how human beings might communicate optimally in a primarily visual medium. At this point we might want to separate ourselves from
the Chomskyan-universalist theories of language—the added
value of the deaf gain is precisely what is different about the
ways in which sign languages are constructed as contrasted
with speech, not the ways in which they are the same. There
is a caveat related to that observation, of course, since the face-
to-face communication of deaf people is constrained by the
functional limitations of the human musculoskeletal system,
but the gain in potential information from reading out this
evolved system is huge. This is true of the reading out of the
genome of any biological species, or the reading out of any
human language and culture. However, the reading out of the
deaf gain is a particularly valuable commodity at this point in
human technological history.

In this regard, the linguistic treatment of ASL and other
sign languages during the latter half of the twentieth century

may have had unintended consequences. As we have seen, part of the program for gaining acceptance of sign languages as bona fide human languages involved adopting the Chomskyan paradigm that they were simply expressions of the universal grammar expressed in a different medium—that their formal structures were dictated, in effect, by a genetically determined language organ in the brain, essentially replicated in each human being. If this were true, a number of conclusions about sign languages and about their use by deaf people should follow.

First, if they were essentially the same as spoken languages, it should be relatively easy to invent signed surrogates for spoken languages. However, the history of deaf education since the late nineteenth century, when natural sign languages were banished from most classrooms worldwide, suggests otherwise. When signing was reintroduced into many educational systems during the latter half of the twentieth century, it tended to be modeled on the dominant spoken language of the country or community. Deaf people have stubbornly resisted efforts to impose sign surrogates for speech, such as signed English, for use in education. What has been attempted through these surrogates is to replicate all of the grammatical features of a spoken language by introducing signed grammatical particles, such as articles, that are absent in sign languages. These surrogates also generally ignore the essential spatial and movement features of signing, which are inherently iconic and indexic.

Second, other systems designed to replicate directly the phonological structures of spoken languages have not been successful in winning support from deaf people. These systems include fingerspelling all the words of a spoken language utterance, as in the so-called Rochester method, or disambiguating the lip movements in speechreading by adding manual cues to the speech stream, as in the method called Cued Speech. This book makes it clear that, if there were a phonological module in the brain cranking out abstract rules of assembly, sign languages should in some respects be like fingerspelling, composed of strings of nicely segmented, arbitrary phonological symbols. However, we know that this is not the case in natural sign languages—they are very stubbornly iconic and will be as iconic as they can be, subject to restraints on what can be presented through direct representation by visible body parts, especially the hands, and on the need for economy in production.

One final unintended consequence of the assertion that all languages are simply the expression of innately determined rules for production and decoding is that proper credit for their invention may not be accruing to their inventors. In a recent ethnography of the French deaf community, Yves Delaporte (2002, 327–344) points out, as we have already seen, that early linguistic descriptions of ASL, beginning in the 1960s, tended to minimize or deny the role of iconicity in signed languages, because of the general prejudice against "mimicry" and "pantomime" as primitive forms of communication (see Armstrong 1999, 65–87). Happily, the linguistic study of sign languages has matured, at least in France (Cuxac 2000; Bouvet 1997) and the United States (Taub 2001; Liddell 2003). Major works are now appearing that describe the grammatical processes of these languages in their own metaphorical, gestural, indexic, and iconic terms and that do justice to the creativity and resourcefulness of the people who create and use them, rather than simply attributing them to a genetically induced language organ.

As we consider the concept of deaf gain, we should also think about how deaf people have been served or disserved by the technology of the day. By doing this, we can get a sense of what they might have to offer those who are interested in maximizing the potential of the revolutionary new communication technologies of the twenty-first century. The revolutionary communication technology that ended the nineteenth and began the twentieth century was the telephone. For deaf people, this technology was enormously disabling—they could not use it if they were profoundly deaf and could not speak, and this fact was used to deny them access to a variety of occupations and to many of the advantages that it gave to hearing people. There is, of course, a double irony here. Alexander Graham Bell, the person generally credited with its invention, was also the late nineteenth century's most prominent advocate of oral education, the suppression of sign language, and the limitation of marriages among deaf people as a means to limit their increase in the population. With the fortune he earned from the telephone, he was able to propagate these messages worldwide, and his prestige as the inventor of the telephone added much weight to his arguments. It was not until the 1960s when a small group of deaf engineers invented the TTY (or TDD-Telecommunications Device for the Deaf), a teletype device connected to a telephone with an acoustic coupler, that deaf people regained at least a part of what the telephone had cost them.

Anything tending to increase social complexity, so that deaf people are forced to interact with strangers away from a small-scale tribal or village society, and are no longer surrounded by close associates and relatives who may be motivated to communicate in sign; and anything, like the telephone, that places a premium on the auditory, has been disabling to deaf people. Modern visual communication technology has begun to reverse the negative trends that began in the late nineteenth century.

This situation has, of course, changed most radically within the past two decades. Televisions must be constructed so as to permit the display of captions, relay services were designed and established so that deaf people could communicate by telephone with hearing people who did not have TDDs, portable texting devices have become almost universal, and so on. But the most revolutionary change has been the introduction of mass availability of visual communication through the Internet, enabled by miniature video cameras. This has resulted in the realization of a dream cherished by the deaf community for more than a century—deaf people can now communicate at a distance, through the Internet, by signing into Webcams connected to computers. They are also being served by video relay systems that involve sign language interpreters who translate signed messages to voice for transmission to nonsigning recipients and vice versa.

But what does all of this progress for deaf people have to do with the concept of deaf gain? The argument here is that the significance of the deaf gain lies in the potential it offers to tap into the knowledge that deaf people have gained over several centuries in how to communicate most effectively and efficiently and apply this knowledge to this vast new visual medium.

The Human Imperative

We alluded above to the potential that language gives us for expediting the process of cultural evolution, and we have seen that this evolutionary process has led to the invention and dissemination of revolutionary new communication technologies. The following list highlights some basic revolutions in human culture and the approximate times of their occurrence, all of them increasing the potential for cultural diversification made possible by increments in information storage and dissemination:

- Invention of language (God knows when, although many, including the current author, have speculated in print)
- Introduction and intergenerational transmission of stone toolmaking traditions (2 million years ago)
- Upper Paleolithic (40,000+ years ago)—qualitative improvements in stone technologies and the first representative art
- Neolithic revolution—invention of agriculture and beginnings of urban civilization, made possible by production of food surpluses and division of labor (10,000 years ago)
- Writing of spoken languages (5,000 years ago)
- Printing—mass production of written material with huge expansion in literacy (500 years ago)
- Internet supported by powerful computers capable of encoding complex visual information (within last 50 years)

The acceleration of cultural evolution is obvious. The key ingredient in the acceleration is probably the advent of nonrandom introduction of new elements (i.e., purposeful invention) some time after the beginning of the Upper Paleolithic. The constant acceleration of the process has become even more evident with the almost instantaneous evolution of the Internet into a worldwide phenomenon penetrating all aspects of government, commerce, and the arts.

What have we learned during the half century of study of sign languages that was launched by Stokoe in 1960? We have learned that the human imperative is not, as has been claimed, to acquire language per se, as defined by a set of abstract criteria—instead, it is to communicate and to communicate using visual symbols whenever those are most efficacious. We have learned that language does not necessarily emerge, all of a piece, from nonlinguistic behavior—at least in the case of sign languages, it can emerge gradually. We have learned from comparative behavioral studies of our closest living relatives that this imperative extends back to our origins as a separate lineage and ultimately a separate species. Finally, we have learned that our capacity to communicate flexibly and effectively in support of cooperative social action has increased exponentially since that lineage began, that it continues to increase, and that exponential rates of increase can be expected into the foreseeable future as we invent and master new communication technologies as yet unimagined.

References

Aldrete, G. S. 1999. *Gestures and acclamations in ancient Rome*. Baltimore: The Johns Hopkins Univ. Press.

Armstrong, D. F. 1984. Scientific and ethical issues in the case for American Sign Language. *Sign Language Studies 43:165–184*.

Armstrong, D. F. 1999. *Original signs: Gesture, sign and the sources of language*. Washington, DC: Gallaudet Univ. Press.

Armstrong, D. F. and S. H. Katz. 1981. Brain laterality in signed and spoken language: A synthetic theory of language use. *Sign Language Studies* 33:319–350.

Armstrong, D. F., W. C. Stokoe, and S. E. Wilcox. 1995. *Gesture and the nature of language*. Cambridge, UK: Cambridge Univ. Press.

Armstrong, D. F., and S. Wilcox. 2003. Origins of sign languages. In *Handbook of Deaf studies, language, and education,* ed. M. Marscharck and P. Spencer, 305–18. Oxford: Oxford Univ. Press.

Armstrong, D. F., and S. Wilcox. 2007. *The gestural origin of language*. New York: Oxford Univ. Press.

Barakat, R. 1975. On ambiguity in Cistercian sign language. *Sign Language Studies* 8:275–289.

Bauman, H-D. 1998. American Sign Language as a medium for poetry: A comparative poetics of sign, speech and writing in twentieth-century American poetry. PhD diss., Binghamton Univ.

Bauman, H-D. 2003. Rede*signing* literature: The cinematic poetics of ASL poetry. *Sign Language Studies* 4(1): 34–47.

Bauman, H-D. 2009. Postscript: Gallaudet protests of 2006 and the myths of in/exclusion. *Sign Language Studies* 10(1): 90–104.

Bauman, H-D, and J. J. Murray. 2009. Reframing: From hearing loss to deaf gain. *Deaf Studies Digital Journal* (fall).

Baynton, D. 2002. The curious death of sign language studies in the nineteenth century. In *The study of signed languages: Essays in honor of William C. Stokoe,* ed. D. F. Armstrong, M. A. Karchmer, and J. V. Van Cleve, 13–34. Washington, DC: Gallaudet Univ. Press.

Bonvillian, J. D., V. L. Ingram, and B. M. McCleary. 2009. Observations on the use of manual signs and gestures in the communicative interactions between Native Americans and Spanish explorers of North America: The accounts of Bernal Díaz del Castillo and Álvar Núñez Cabeza de Vaca. *Sign Language Studies* 9(2): 132–65.

Bouvet, Danielle. 1997. *Le corps et la métaphore dans les langues gestuelles: A la recherche des modes de production des signes.* Paris: L'Harmattan.

Branson, J., D. Miller, and I. J. Masaja. 1996. Everyone here speaks sign language too: A deaf village in Bali, Indonesia. In *Multicultural aspects of sociolinguistics in deaf communities,* ed. C. Lucas, 39–57. Washington, DC: Gallaudet Univ. Press.

Bruce, S. G. 2007. *Silence and sign language in medieval monasticism: The Cluniac tradition ca. 900–1200.* New York: Cambridge Univ. Press.

Carty, B., S. Macready, and E. E. Sayers. 2009. A grave and gracious woman: Deaf people and signed languages in colonial New England. *Sign Language Studies* 9(3): 287–323.

Chomsky, N. 1995. *The minimalist program.* Cambridge, MA: MIT Press.

Christiansen, J. B. 2009. The 2006 protest at Gallaudet University: Reflections and explanations. *Sign Language Studies* 10(1): 69–89.

Cuxac, C. 2000. La langue des signes française; les voies de l'iconicité. *Faits de langues* 15–16. Paris: Ophrys.

De Jorio, A. 2002. *Gesture in Naples and gesture in classical antiquity.* Trans. by A. Kendon. Bloomington: Indiana Univ. Press. (Orig. pub. 1832.)

Delaporte, Y. 2002. *Les sourds: C'est comme ça.* Paris: Editions de la Maison des Sciences de L'Homme.

Engberg-Pedersen, E. 1993. *Space in Danish Sign Language: The semantics and morphosyntax of the use of space in a visual language.* Hamburg: Signum-Verlag.

Farnell, B. 1995. *Do you see what I mean: Plains Indian sign talk and the embodiment of action.* Austin, TX: Univ. of Texas Press.

Fouts, R., and S. T. Mills. 1997. *Next of kin.* New York: William Morrow.

Fischer, R. 2002. The study of natural sign language in 18th-century France. *Sign Language Studies* 2(4): 391–406.

Fox, M. 2007. *Talking hands: What sign language reveals about the mind.* New York: Simon and Schuster.

Fox Tree, E. 2009. Meemul Tziij: An indigenous sign language complex of Mesoamerica. *Sign Language Studies* 9(3): 324–66.

Frishberg, N. 1975. Arbitrariness and iconicity: Historical change in American Sign Language. *Language* 51:699–719.

Fusellier-Souza, I. 2006. Emergence and development of signed languages: From a semiogenetic point of view. *Sign Language Studies* 7(1): 30–56.

Gardner, R. E., B. T. Gardner, and T. E. Van Cantfort, eds. 1989. *Teaching sign language to chimpanzees.* Albany, NY: State Univ. of New York Press.

Gardner, R. E., B. T. Gardner, and S. G. Nichols. 1989. The infant Loulis learns signs from cross-fostered chimpanzees. In *Teaching sign language to chimpanzees,* eds. R. E. Gardner, B. T. Gardner, and T. E. Van Cantfort, 280–92. Albany, NY: State Univ. of New York Press.

Givón, T. 1989. *Mind, code and context: Essays in pragmatics.* Hillsdale, NJ: Lawrence Erlbaum.

Givón, T. 1998. On the co-evolution of language, mind, and brain. *Evolution of Communication* 2(1): 45–116.

Goffman. E. 1987. *Gender advertisements.* New York: Harper and Row.

Goodall, J. 1965. Chimpanzees of the Gombe Stream Reserve. In *Primate behavior,* ed. I. Devore. New York: Holt, Rinehart, Winston.

Graham, S. 1854. *Lectures on the science of human life.* London: Horsell, Aldine Chambers.

Groce, N. E. 1985. *Everyone here spoke sign language: Hereditary deafness on Martha's Vineyard.* Cambridge, MA: Harvard Univ. Press.

Harnad, S. R., H. D. Steklis, and J. Lancaster, eds. 1976. *Origins and evolution of language and speech.* New York: The New York Academy of Sciences.

Harrison, K. D. 2007. *When languages die: The extinction of the world's languages and the erosion of human knowledge.* New York: Oxford Univ. Press.

Hebard, G. R. 1999. *Sacajawea.* Mansfield Centre, CT: Overland Trails Press. (Orig. pub. 1933.)

Hertz, R. 1973. The pre-eminence of the right hand: A study in religious polarity. In *Right and left,* trans. and ed. R. Needham. Chicago: Univ. of Chicago Press. (Orig. pub. 1909.)

106 | REFERENCES

Hewes, G. W. 1973. Primate communication and the gestural origin of language. *Current Anthropology* 14:5–24.

Hewes, G. W. 1976. The current status of the gestural theory of language origins. *Annals of the New York Academy of Sciences* 280:482–504.

Hewes, G. W. 1996. A history of the study of language origins and the gestural primacy hypothesis. In *Handbook of human symbolic evolution,* ed. A. Lock and C. R. Peters, 571–95. Oxford: Clarendon Press.

Hockett, C. 1960. The origin of speech. *Scientific American* 203:88–111.

Holzer, H. 2004. *Lincoln at Cooper Union.* New York: Simon and Schuster.

Hopkins, W.D. 1999. Heritability of hand preference in chimpanzees (*Pan troglodytes*): Evidence from a partial interspecies cross-fostering study. *Journal of Comparative Psychology* 113(3): 307–13.

Hopkins, W. D., M. J. Wesley, M. K. Izard, M. Hook, and S. J. Schapiro. 2004. Chimpanzees (*Pan troglodytes*) are predominantly right-handed: Replication in three populations of apes. *Behavioral Neuroscience* 118(3): 659–63.

Horwitz, T. 2008. *A voyage long and strange.* New York: Henry Holt.

Johnson, R. E. 1992. Sign language, culture, and community in a traditional Yucatec Maya village. *Sign Language Studies* 73:461–74.

Johnston, Trevor. 2004. W(h)ither the deaf community? Population, genetics, and the future of Australian Sign Language. *American Annals of the Deaf* 148:358–75.

Jowett, D. 1901. *The dialogues of Plato,* vol. 1. New York: Charles Scribner's Sons.

Kendon, A. 1988. *Sign languages of Aboriginal Australia: Cultural, semiotic, and communicative perspectives.* New York: Cambridge Univ. Press.

Kendon, A. 2002. Historical observations on the relationship between research on sign languages and language origins theory. In *The study of signed languages: Essays in honor of William C. Stokoe,* ed. D. F. Armstrong, M. A. Karchmer, and J.V. Van Cleve, 13–34. Washington, DC: Gallaudet Univ. Press.

Kendon, A. 2004. *Gesture: Visible action as utterance.* New York: Cambridge Univ. Press.

Kimura, D. 1981. Neural mechanisms in manual signing. *Sign Language Studies* 33:291–312.

King, B. J. 2003. Alternative pathways for the evolution of gesture: Review of M. C. Corballis, *From hand to mouth*. *Sign Language Studies* 4(1): 68–82.

King, B. J. 2004. *The dynamic dance: Nonvocal communication in African great apes*. Cambridge, MA: Harvard Univ. Press.

King, B. J. 2008. ME . . . ME . . . WASHOE: An Appreciation. *Sign Language Studies* 8(3): 315–24.

King, B. J., and S. G. Shanker. 1997. The expulsion of primates from the garden of language: Review of W. Noble and I. Davidson, *Human evolution, language, and mind*. *Evolution of Communication* 1(1): 59–99.

Klima, E., and U. Bellugi. 1979. *The signs of language*. Cambridge, MA: Harvard Univ. Press.

Kuschel, R. 1973. The silent inventor: The creation of a sign language by the only deaf-mute on a Polynesian island. *Sign Language Studies* 3:1–27.

Lane, H. 1976. *The wild boy of Aveyron*. Cambridge, MA: Harvard Univ. Press.

Lane, H. 1984. *When the mind hears: A history of the deaf.* New York: Random House.

Lang, H. 2003. Perspectives on the history of deaf education. In *Oxford handbook of deaf studies, language, and education*, ed. M. Marschark and P. E. Spencer, 9–20. Oxford: Oxford Univ. Press.

Liddell, S. K. 2003. *Grammar, gesture, and meaning in American Sign Language*. New York: Cambridge Univ. Press.

Mallery, G. 1881. *Sign language among North American Indians compared with that among other peoples and deaf-mutes*. First annual report of the Bureau of Ethnology to the secretary of the Smithsonian Institution. Washington, DC: GPO, 1879–1880, pages 263–552. Retrieved from http://www.gutenberg.org/files/17451/17451-h/17451-h.htm.

Marzke, M. W., and R. F. Marzke. 2000. Evolution of the human hand: Approaches to acquiring, analyzing, and interpreting the anatomical evidence. *Journal of Anatomy* 197:121–40.

McBurney S. L. 2001. William Stokoe and the discipline of sign language linguistics. *Historiographica Linguistica* 28(1/2): 143–86.

Meissner, M., and S. Phillpot. 1975. The sign language of saw mill workers in British Columbia. *Sign Language Studies* 9:291–308.

Munn, N. 1973. *Walbiri iconography.* Ithaca, NY: Cornell Univ. Press.

Myklebust, H. 1957. *The psychology of deafness.* New York: Grune and Stratton.

Nakamura, K. 2006. Creating and contesting signs in contemporary Japan: Language ideologies, identity, and community in flux. *Sign Language Studies* 7(1): 11–29.

Napier, J. 1970. *The roots of mankind.* Washington, DC: Smithsonian Institution Press.

Needham, R., ed. 1973. *Right and left.* Chicago: Univ. of Chicago Press.

Neisser, A. 1983. *The other side of silence.* New York: Alfred A. Knopf.

Padden, C., and T. Humphries. 1988. *Deaf in America: Voices from a culture.* Cambridge: Harvard Univ. Press.

Pinker, S. 1994. *The language instinct.* New York: William Morrow.

Plann, S. 1993. Pedro Ponce de León: Myth and reality. In *Deaf history unveiled: Interpretations from the new scholarship*, ed. J. V. Van Cleve. Washington, DC: Gallaudet Univ. Press.

Poizner, H., E. S. Klima, and U. Bellugi. 1987. *What the hands reveal about the brain.* Cambridge, MA: MIT Press.

Premack, D. 1986. *Gavagai! Or the future history of the animal language controversy.* Cambridge, MA: MIT Press.

Rée, J. 1999. *I see a voice.* New York: Metropolitan Books.

Reynolds, V. 1965. Some behavioral comparisons between the chimpanzee and the mountain gorilla in the wild. *American Anthropologist* 67: 691–705.

Rosenfeld, S. 2001. *A revolution in language: The problem of signs in late eighteenth-century France.* Stanford, CA: Stanford Univ. Press.

Sacks, O. 1989. *Seeing voices.* Berkeley: Univ. of California Press.

Sandler, W., I. Meir, C. Padden, and M. Aronoff. 2005. The emergence of grammar: Systematic structure in a new language. In *Proceedings of the National Academy of Sciences* 102(7): 2661–65.

Sapir, E. 1921. *Language.* New York: Harcourt, Brace, and World.

Saussy, H., J. Stalling, and L. Klein, eds. 2008. *The Chinese written character as a medium for poetry by Ernest Fenollosa and Ezra Pound, a critical edition.* New York: Fordham Univ. Press.

Savage-Rumbaugh, E. S., B. J. Wilkerson, and R. Bakerman. 1977. Spontaneous gestural communication among conspecifics in the pygmy chimpanzee (*Pan paniscus*). In *Progress in ape research,* ed. G. H. Bourne, 91–116. New York: Academic Press.

Schaller, G. 1965. The behavior of the mountain gorilla. In *Primate behavior,* ed. I. DeVore. New York: Holt, Rinehart, and Winston.

Schuchman, J. S. 2004. The silent film era: Silent films, NAD films, and the Deaf community's response. *Sign Language Studies* 4(3): 231–38.

Senghas, A., S. Kita, and A. Ozyurek. 2004. Children creating core properties of language: Evidence from an emerging sign language in Nicaragua. *Science* 305:1779–82.

Slobin, D. I. 2008. Breaking the molds: Signed languages and the nature of human languages. *Sign Language Studies* 8(2): 114–30.

Stokoe, W. C. 1960. Sign language structure: An outline of the visual communication systems of the American deaf. *In Studies in Linguistics: Occasional Papers 8.* Buffalo, NY: University of Buffalo Department of Anthropology and Linguistics.

Stokoe, W. C. 1991. Semantic phonology. *Sign Language Studies* 71:99–106.

Stokoe, W. C. 2001. *Language in hand.* Washington, DC: Gallaudet Univ. Press.

Stokoe, W. C., D. C. Casterline, and C. G. Croneberg. 1965. *A dictionary of American Sign Language on linguistic principles.* Washington, DC: Gallaudet College Press.

Stokoe, W. C., and V. Volterra, eds. 1985. *Proceedings of the third international symposium on sign language research.* Silver Spring, MD: Linstok Press.

Supalla, T. 2004. The validity of the Gallaudet lecture films. *Sign Language Studies* 4(3): 261–292.

Suzuki, A. 1969. An ecological study of chimpanzees in a savanna woodland. *Primates* 10:197–225.

Tanner, J. E., and R. W. Byrne. 1996. Representation of action through iconic gesture in a captive lowland gorilla. *Current Anthropology* 37:12–73.

Tanner, J. E., and R. W. Byrne. 1999. The development of spontaneous gestural communication in a group of zoo-living lowland gorillas. In *The mentalities of gorillas and orangutans,* ed. S. T. Parker, R. W. Mitchell, and H. L. Miles, 211–39. New York: Cambridge Univ. Press.

Taub, S. 2001. *Language from the body: Iconicity and metaphor in American Sign Language.* Cambridge: Cambridge Univ. Press.

Terrace, H. S., L. A. Petitto, R. J. Sanders, and T. G. Bever. 1979. Can an ape create a sentence? *Science* 206:891–900.

Umiker-Sebeok, D. J., and T.A. Sebeok, eds. 1978. *Aboriginal sign languages of the Americas and Australia*. New York: Plenum Press.

Van Cleve, J. V., and B. A. Crouch. 1989. *A place of their own: Creating the deaf community in America*. Washington, DC: Gallaudet Univ. Press.

Van Lawick-Goodall. J. 1971. *In the shadow of man*. Boston: Houghton Mifflin.

Wallman, J. 1992. *Aping language*. Cambridge: Cambridge Univ. Press.

Washabaugh, W. 1986. *Five fingers for survival*. Ann Arbor, MI: Karoma Publishers.

Wescott, R., ed. 1974. *Language origins*. Silver Spring, MD: Linstok Press.

West, L. 1960. The sign language: An analysis. PhD diss., Indiana University.

Wilcox, P. P. 2000. *Metaphor in American Sign Language*. Washington, DC: Gallaudet Univ. Press.

Wilcox, S. 1996. Hands and bodies, minds and souls: Or, how a sign linguist learned to stop worrying and love gesture. Paper presented at the Workshop on Integrating Language and Gesture, University of Delaware, Newark.

Wilson, F. 1998. *The hand: How its use shapes the brain, language, and human culture*. New York: Pantheon Books.

Index

language: defined, 13–19; duality of patterning in, 17, 18; as encoding mechanism, 93–94; as genetic, 16–17, 53, 70, 74, 78; structures, 16, 66; theories on origins of, 33, 69, 76, 81–82; visual bases of, 85–101; visucentric view of, 87–88. *See also* gestures; signing systems

Language: An Introduction to the Study of Speech (Sapir), 64–65

language faculty, 64–84; biological basis and structure of sign languages, 83–84; modern linguistics of sign language, 64–75; origin and evolution of, 69; signing apes, 75–83

Language in Hand (Stokoe), 74

The Language Instinct (Pinker), 53, 81

Language Origins (Wescott), 69

Latin lexicon incorporated into English language, 39–40

Lewis and Clark, 56

Lincoln, Abraham, 22, 37

lingua franca, sign language as, 18, 48, 55, 57

linguistic evolution, 94–95

Linguistics Research Laboratory, 67

Linstok Press, 69

LSF. *See* French Sign Language (Langue des Signes Française)

Lucretius, 20

Macready, S., 32

mainstreaming of deaf and hard of hearing students, 44

Mallery, Garrick, 57–58

"mano cornuta" (horned hand), 24–25, 24*f*

Martha's Vineyard, sign language of, 34, 46–47

Masaja, I. J., 47

Mather, Increase, 32

Mayan deaf community, 48, 49*f,* 50

McBurney, Susan Lloyd, 74

Meemul Tziij (Mayan sign language), 48, 49*f,* 50

Mesoamerican Mayan deaf community. *See* Mayan deaf community

metaphor, 10, 25, 62, 86, 97

A Midsummer Night's Dream (Shakespeare), 9

Miller, D., 47

Missouri River, Lakota sign for, 57–58

mobility, in deaf vs. blind, 11

monastic signing systems, 23, 27–29, 28*f,* 64–65

Montana, Indians of, 57

morphemes, 17

morphology, 16

Munn, N., 59–60

Nakota or Assiniboine Indians, 57

Napier, John, 15–16

National Association of the Deaf (NAD), 40

nativist school of linguistics, 16

natural selection, process of, 93

natural sign languages, 96, 97

Neapolitan gestural system, 23–24, 25, 26*f*

Needham, Rodney, 4

neurology: adaptations for signed languages, 83–84; cross-modal association, 10; of handedness and language, 3–4; underpinnings of ASL, 74

Nicaraguan sign language (NSL), 50, 51–53

"Nim Chimpsky" project, 77

Observations of a Deaf-Mute (Desloges), 33–34

OK gesture, 15

oralists, 64

Padden, Carol, 30–31, 40–41

pantomime and pantomime dance, 25–26, 97

parietal/occipital/temporal area (POT), 10

phonemes, 17

phonology, 16

Pinker, Steven, 16–18, 53, 75, 81